Conte

Success Tips for Cakes   3
Everything you need to know about baking, frosting,
decorating, storing and freezing cakes

Elegant Cakes & Tortes   8
Cakes and tortes for parties and special occasions,
sophisticated in taste and appearance yet simple to
prepare

Easy Cakes for Everyday   22
Sure to become family favorites, these cakes bake up fast
and easy for a change of pace

Children's Party Cakes   42
An assortment of cakes and cupcakes with easy-to-do
decorations, each one guaranteed to delight children

Holiday Baking   54
A delicious collection of cookies, cakes, desserts and
breads—perfect for holiday entertaining

Desserts   64
Luscious cheesecakes, delectable fruit desserts and rich
chocolate creations—all beginning with Duncan Hines
Cake Mixes

Cookies and Bars   74
All-time favorites, like Lemon Bars and Ribbon Cookies,
plus new ideas, like Wheat Germ Cookies and Coconut
Mallow Fudge Squares

Muffins, Loaves & Coffee Cakes   82
The quick-and-easy way to enjoy fresh-baked breads for
breakfast, coffee breaks or any time of the day

Index   94

Photography by Cy DeCosse Creative, Minneapolis.

Manufactured in Yugoslavia
ISBN 0-88176-476-0

Success Tips For Cakes

BAKING CAKES

Prepare the Baking Pans

Be sure to use the correct pan size for each recipe, which usually is stamped on the bottom of the pan. An incorrect pan size affects the baking time and may cause your baked product to rise improperly, shrink, or overflow the pan.

Shiny metal pans are preferred for even baking. Oven-proof glass pans may be used also, but reduce the oven temperature by 25°F.

Follow recipe instructions for preparing pans. When an ungreased pan is specified, the use of a greased pan may ruin your cake.

When a recipe calls for greased and floured pans, do this step before mixing the batter. It is important to bake the batter immediately after mixing. Grease each pan generously using at least ½ tablespoon of shortening for each pan. Apply the shortening evenly with a brush or wax paper. Sprinkle flour in pan and tilt to distribute the flour evenly.

Mix the Batter

Mixing batter is the easiest part of baking a cake. An electric mixer will do most of the work for you. Usually, the first step is simply to blend all the ingredients just until they are moistened; use the mixer on low speed or combine the ingredients by hand with a wooden spoon.

The second step is to beat the ingredients, scraping down the sides of the bowl often with a rubber spatula, until enough air has been incorporated to make the cake rise high and fluffy. Use the speed recommended on your portable or standard mixer.

Follow the beating time indicated in the recipe or on the cake mix package, making sure you do not underbeat or overbeat. (Underbeating does not incorporate enough air; overbeating releases the air previously incorporated and undoes your work.) Set your kitchen timer for perfect accuracy.

Always bake cakes immediately after mixing the batter.

Greasing pans (left), flouring pans (right)

Bake layers staggered in oven (left), testing for doneness (center), cool on racks (right)

Bake

First, remember to preheat your oven to the temperature specified in the recipe or on the cake mix package for a full 15 to 20 minutes.

Baking at the proper oven temperature is extremely important, since overbaking or underbaking is the most common cause of less-than-perfect cakes. If you doubt the reliability of your oven thermostat, check it with an oven thermometer. Simply set the oven and place the thermometer inside for 20 to 30 minutes. If they do not agree, the oven setting must be adjusted accordingly.

Even heating is important, too. If two oven racks are used, stagger the pans to avoid having one pan directly over another. If a single rack is used, position it so that the pans are as near the center of the oven as possible. Do not allow pans to touch each other or sides of oven. Do not open the oven door until you think cake is done; heat is lost quickly.

A kitchen timer, if your oven thermostat is accurate, will tell you approximately when the cake should be done. Before the cake is removed from the oven, however, it must be tested for doneness.

To test cakes insert a toothpick in the center. When done, the toothpick will come out perfectly clean.

Cooling Cakes

Cool layer cakes in pans on wire racks for at least 10 minutes, but not more than 20 minutes. Then gently loosen sides of cake with a spatula.

To remove a layer cake from the pan, wrap a dish towel around a wire rack (so it won't leave an imprint), place it on top of the pan, and invert the pan and rack together. Remove the pan and your cake will be upside down on the protected rack.

Then, to get the cake right-side-up, place another rack on the bottom of the cake and turn over both racks with the cake between them. When the protected rack is removed, your cake will be right-side-up on a wire rack, where it should stay to finish cooling. Always use wire racks so that air can circulate evenly around the cake.

For a cake that is rolled, like a jelly-roll cake, turn out the cake and roll it in a towel while still warm enough to be shaped. When cool, it can be unrolled, spread with a filling, and rerolled without the towel.

Frost with small spatula (left), splitting layers (center), doily decoration (right)

FROSTING CAKES

Before frosting any cake, let it cool completely. Never frost a warm cake unless the recipe directs you to do so. Brush off any loose crumbs, which tend to mix in with the frosting. If necessary, a thin coating of frosting, applied first, will seal in any remaining crumbs. For the best-looking cakes, swirl the frosting in a decorative way as it is applied. The best tool for frosting is a small metal spatula.

To catch any drips and keep the cake plate neat, place four pieces of wax paper under edges of the bottom layer, which will slide out after the cake is frosted.

To frost a 2-layer cake, place one layer upside-down on a plate, and spread about one-fourth of the frosting on top. Then place the second layer right-side up on top of the frosted layer. Frost the sides first with about two-thirds of the remaining frosting; then frost the top.

Some recipes require the cutting of layers into two thin layers before applying the frosting. To split a layer evenly, measure its height with a ruler and mark off the center point with toothpicks inserted around the cake. Then cut across the tops of the toothpicks with a long serrated knife, using a sawing motion.

DECORATING CAKES

Here are some simple cake decorating ideas that will dress up your cakes quickly and easily.

Decorate an unfrosted cake by placing a paper doily on top and sifting confectioners' sugar heavily over the doily. Lift the doily carefully and you will have an imprint of its design on the cake.

Use the tip of a knife to score the top of a chocolate or white frosted cake into six or eight triangles. Fill alternate triangles with chopped walnuts, peanuts, cashews, or pistachio nuts.

Tint shredded coconut with one or two drops of food coloring dissolved in a teaspoon of water. Shake in a jar. Create several colors of shredded coconut and sprinkle them like confetti, over the cake.

Melt semisweet chocolate, spread in circle between pieces of wax paper, and let harden in the refrigerator. Then remove one sheet of wax paper, cut the chocolate into wedges, and lift them off with a small

Chocolate wedge decoration (left), chocolate drizzle decoration (center), storing with cooked frosting (right)

spatula. Decorate the top of your cake with the wedges.

Using a teaspoon, drizzle melted chocolate in parallel lines across a white frosted sheet cake. Then draw a knife down through the lines to create a feathered, criss-cross effect.

To decorate truly fancy cakes, you will need a pastry bag fitted with various decorator tips. With a little practice, you will be able to make lovely designs. Be careful not to fill the bag more than half full and to apply even pressure. (A toss-away decorator bag can be improvised by rolling and taping a 15-inch triangle of parchment paper and snipping off the tip.)

AT HIGH ALTITUDE

If you live in an area above 3500 feet, you must adjust the recipes according to the specific instructions on each Duncan Hines Cake Mix package.

High altitude baked goods have a tendency to stick to the pan. Be sure to grease the pans generously before dusting with flour. Fill the pans only half full with batter; otherwise, high altitude cakes may overflow the pan. Use eggs that are cold, not at room temperature.

For answers to other high altitude baking problems, contact the home economics department of your state college, the state agricultural extension service, the home service department of your local utility company, or Colorado State University, Fort Collins, Colorado 80521.

STORING CAKES

Cakes, except fruitcakes, are at their best the day they are made. But, if stored properly, most cakes will remain fresh for several days.

Unfrosted cakes must be cooled completely before being wrapped and stored, or they will become soggy. Cakes with creamy frostings may be stored in a cake keeper, under an inverted bowl, or loosely covered with aluminum foil or plastic wrap.

Cakes with cooked-type frostings do not store well. But leftovers may be stored in a cake keeper or under an inverted bowl, provided a knife or spatula is inserted under the edge to keep it from being airtight.

Whipped cream cakes (either topped or filled), cheesecakes, or cakes containing cream cheese, sour cream, or yogurt must be refrigerated.

FREEZING & THAWING

Unfrosted cakes freeze well for up to 4 months. Place them on cardboard and wrap them in aluminum foil or plastic wrap. Thaw at room temperature, wrapped or unwrapped.

Frosted cakes can be frozen about 2 months, wrapped in aluminum foil or plastic wrap. To prevent the frosting from sticking to the wrapping, freeze the cake before wrapping it. Or insert toothpicks in the sides and top of the cake to hold the wrapping away, making sure not to puncture the wrapping. Thaw at room temperature.

Whipped cream cakes should be treated like frosted cakes, and may be frozen for the same length of time. Thaw in the refrigerator for several hours. Or thaw individual servings on plates for 5 minutes.

Cakes with fruit or custard fillings are not recommended for freezing; they become soggy when thawed.

TIPS FOR ANGEL FOOD CAKES

Follow the package directions carefully. Much thorough testing has gone into developing them.

Be sure the bowl, beaters, and spatula are really clean! Even the smallest trace of grease on them will keep egg whites from whipping properly.

For the best cake, beat the egg whites until they hold a very stiff peak. Test the egg whites by cutting through to the bottom of the mixture with a wide spatula—egg whites should hold the trench shape and not run together at the bottom of the bowl.

Bake on the lowest oven rack position but not on the floor of the oven. If there are two racks, remove the top one. Duncan Hines Angel Food Cakes rise high and need plenty of room. To cool, hang the pan upside down on a funnel or bottle at least 1½ hours. To remove cake from pan, loosen edges with knife.

Preparing for freezing (left), egg whites for angel food cake (right)

Elegant Cakes & Tortes

LUSCIOUS CHOCOLATE PARTY CAKE

1 package Duncan Hines Deluxe Devil's Food Cake Mix
3 large eggs
½ cup Crisco Oil or Puritan Oil
1⅓ cups water
2 ounces (2 squares) unsweetened chocolate
10 tablespoons sugar
2 tablespoons water
4 large egg yolks, slightly beaten
2 tablespoons rum
1 cup (2 sticks) butter or margarine, softened
2 cups confectioners' sugar
4 large egg whites
1 cup whipping cream
½ teaspoon vanilla extract
Chocolate curls
Red maraschino cherries

1. Preheat oven to 350°F. Grease and flour two 8×1½-inch round layer pans.

2. Combine dry cake mix, 3 eggs, oil and 1⅓ cups water in large mixer bowl. Mix, bake and cool cake as directed on package. Chill cooled layers to make splitting easier. Split each cake layer into two thin layers.

3. Combine chocolate, ¼ cup sugar and 2 tablespoons water in top of double boiler. Heat over hot water until chocolate melts. Stir to blend, then stir a little hot mixture into 4 yolks. Return yolk mixture to double boiler top. Cook and stir until thick and smooth, about 3 minutes. Remove from heat. Cool.

4. Stir rum into cooled chocolate mixture. Cream butter and confectioners' sugar until light and fluffy. Fold in chocolate mixture. Beat 4 egg whites until frothy. Gradually add ¼ cup sugar, beating until stiff peaks form. Fold in chocolate mixture. Refrigerate 1 hour or until firm enough to spread. Spread between layers and on sides of cake. Do not spread over top layer. Refrigerate overnight or until firm.

5. To serve, whip cream until stiff. Fold in remaining 2 tablespoons sugar and vanilla extract. Spread over top of cake. Decorate with pecan halves, chocolate curls and maraschino cherries. Store in refrigerator.

16 servings

PINEAPPLE BLITZ TORTE

1 package Duncan Hines Deluxe Pineapple Cake Mix

4 large eggs, separated

⅓ cup Crisco Oil or Puritan Oil

1¼ cups water

¾ cup plus 1 tablespoon sugar

¼ cup chopped nuts

½ cup whipping cream

½ teaspoon vanilla extract

½ cup well-drained crushed pineapple

1. Preheat oven to 350°F. Grease and flour two 9×1½-inch round layer pans.

2. Combine dry cake mix, egg yolks, oil and water in large mixer bowl. Mix cake as directed on package. Divide batter evenly in pans.

3. Beat egg whites until frothy. Gradually add ¾ cup sugar, beating until stiff peaks form. Carefully spread meringue over batter. Sprinkle with nuts.

4. Bake at 350°F for 30 to 35 minutes. Cool in pans on racks 15 minutes; remove layers from pans and cool completely, meringue-side-up, on racks.

5. For filling, beat cream until stiff; beat in 1 tablespoon sugar and vanilla extract. Fold in crushed pineapple.

6. Place one cake layer, meringue-side-down, on plate; spread with filling. Place second layer, meringue-side-up, on top. Refrigerate until ready to serve.

12 to 16 servings

OPEN HOUSE RIBBON TORTE

1 package Duncan Hines
Deluxe Fudge Marble
Cake Mix
3 large eggs
⅓ cup Crisco Oil or Puritan
Oil

1¼ cups water
1 cup whipping cream
1 cup milk
1 package (4-serving-size)
chocolate instant pudding
and pie filling mix

1. Preheat oven to 350°F. Grease and flour two 8×1½- or 9×1½-inch round layer pans.

2. Combine dry cake mix, eggs, oil and water in large mixer bowl. Mix as directed on package but do not add contents of small packet. Turn half of batter (about 2½ cups) into one pan. Blend contents of small packet into remaining batter and turn into remaining pan.

3. Bake and cool layers as directed on package. Chill cooled layers to make splitting easier. Split each layer into two thin layers.

4. Whip cream until stiff. Blend in milk and pudding mix. Let set 1 minute.

5. Place one chocolate layer on plate. Spread one-fourth pudding mixture over layer. Top with remaining layers, alternating light and dark layers and spreading pudding mixture between layers. Frost top layer with pudding mixture. Refrigerate until ready to serve.

12 to 16 servings

STRAWBERRIES ROMANOFF ON ANGEL SLICES

1 package Duncan Hines Deluxe Angel Food Cake Mix
1⅓ cups water
1½ pints fresh strawberries, hulled and halved lengthwise
⅓ cup orange juice
3 tablespoons orange-flavored liqueur
2 tablespoons sugar
1 cup whipping cream
½ teaspoon vanilla extract

1. Preheat oven to 375°F.

2. Prepare cake with water as directed on package. Pour batter into ungreased 10-inch tube pan. Cut through batter with knife or spatula to remove large air bubbles.

3. Bake at 375°F for 30 to 40 minutes or until top crust is golden brown, firm and dry. Do not underbake. To cool, hang pan upside down on funnel or bottle at least 1½ hours.

4. Place strawberries in bowl. Combine orange juice, 2 tablespoons of the liqueur and sugar; pour over strawberries. Cover with plastic wrap. Refrigerate, occasionally spooning liquid over strawberries.

5. Beat whipping cream until soft peaks form. Beat in remaining 1 tablespoon liqueur and vanilla extract. Beat until thick. Refrigerate until ready to use.

6. To serve, cut cake into slices. Spoon some strawberries and liquid over cake slices; top with whipped cream.

12 to 16 servings

Variation: Prepare cake and strawberries as for Strawberries Romanoff on Angel Slices, but omit whipped cream topping and top with following mixture: Beat 1 cup chilled whipping cream in large bowl until slightly thickened. Add 2 tablespoons orange-flavored liqueur and ½ teaspoon vanilla extract. Beat until soft peaks form. Fold in ½ cup chilled dairy sour cream. Beat until cream is thick and holds its shape. Spoon cream over strawberries and cake slices.

SWEET CHOCOLATE MOUSSE CAKE

1 package Duncan Hines
  Butter Recipe
  Fudge Cake Mix
3 large eggs
½ cup (1 stick) butter or
  margarine, softened

¾ cup water
2 packages (4 ounces each)
  sweet baking chocolate
¼ cup water
6 large eggs, separated
1 teaspoon vanilla extract

1. Preheat oven to 375°F. Grease and flour two 8×1½-inch round layer pans.

2. Combine dry cake mix, 3 eggs, butter and ¾ cup water in large mixer bowl. Mix, bake and cool cake as directed on package.

3. Combine chocolate and ¼ cup water in top of double boiler. Heat over simmering, not boiling, water until melted. Cool slightly.

4. Beat 6 egg whites in large bowl until stiff, not dry, peaks form.

5. Beat 6 egg yolks in large bowl until thick (about 3 minutes); beat in chocolate mixture and vanilla extract. Fold in beaten egg whites. Refrigerate 30 minutes.

6. Cut each cooled layer into 8 wedges and arrange in 9-inch round layer pan so wedges are separated. Pour half of mousse over cake in each pan. Gently spread to fill spaces between wedges. Refrigerate until set.

16 servings

VIENNESE CHERRY CHEESE TORTE

1 *package Duncan Hines Butter Recipe Golden Cake Mix*
3 *large eggs*
½ *cup (1 stick) butter or margarine, softened*
⅔ *cup water*

1 *package (8 ounces) plus 1 package (3 ounces) cream cheese, softened*
⅔ *cup sugar*
¼ *teaspoon ground nutmeg*
2 *tablespoons milk*
1 *can (21 ounces) cherry pie filling*

1. Preheat oven to 375°F. Grease and flour two 8×1½- or 9×1½-inch round layer pans.

2. Combine dry cake mix, eggs, butter and water in large mixer bowl. Mix, bake and cool as directed on package. Refrigerate layers to make splitting easier. Split each cake into 2 thin layers.

3. For filling, beat cream cheese, sugar, nutmeg and milk until smooth.

4. Place one layer on cake plate. Spread with ½ cup cream cheese filling; top with ½ cup cherry filling. Repeat layers, ending with cake layer. Spread remaining cream cheese filling over top layer and top with remaining cherry filling. Refrigerate until ready to serve.

12 to 16 servings

ELEGANT ANGEL TORTE

1 package Duncan Hines
Deluxe Angel Food Cake
Mix
1⅓ cups water
2 cups whipping cream
¼ cup chocolate syrup
1 tablespoon sugar

⅓ cup orange marmalade
6 red maraschino cherries
with stems, if desired
6 pecan halves, if desired
¼ cup chocolate curls, if
desired

1. Preheat oven to 375°F.

2. Prepare cake with water as directed on package. Pour batter into ungreased 10-inch tube pan. Cut through batter with knife or spatula to remove large air bubbles.

3. Bake at 375°F for 30 to 40 minutes or until top crust is golden brown, firm and dry. Do not underbake. To cool, hang pan upside down on funnel or bottle at least 1½ hours.

4. Slice cooled cake crosswise into four 1-inch layers.

5. Whip cream until stiff. Beat in chocolate syrup and sugar. Place bottom cake slice on serving plate; spread with ⅓ cup whipped cream. Top with next layer; spread with orange marmalade. Top with next layer; spread with ⅓ cup whipped cream. Add final layer. Frost sides and top with remaining whipped cream. Decorate with cherries, pecans and chocolate curls.   *12 to 16 servings*

CHOCOLAT AU RHUM

1 package Duncan Hines
   Deluxe Devil's Food Cake
   Mix
4 large eggs
½ cup Crisco Oil or Puritan
   Oil
1¼ cups water
1 package (4-serving-size)
   chocolate instant pudding
   and pie filling mix

¾ cup light corn syrup
¾ cup light rum or ¾ cup
   water plus ½ to ¾
   teaspoon rum extract
1 cup whipping cream
2 tablespoons sugar
½ teaspoon vanilla extract
   Grated chocolate, if
   desired

1. Preheat oven to 350°F. Grease and flour 10-inch tube pan.

2. Combine dry cake mix, eggs, oil, water and pudding mix in large mixer bowl. Mix cake as directed on package. Turn batter into pan and spread evenly.

3. Bake at 350°F for 50 to 60 minutes. Cool in pan 15 minutes.

4. Blend corn syrup and rum. Slowly pour half of syrup over top of warm cake in pan. Let cake cool completely, then remove from pan; turn upside down on serving platter and pour remaining syrup over cake. Let stand several hours.

5. To serve, beat cream until stiff; beat in sugar and vanilla extract. Slice cake and top with whipped cream. Sprinkle grated chocolate over whipped cream.

12 to 16 servings

Tip: *Underbaking or overbaking is the most common cause of less-than-perfect cakes. If you doubt the reliability of your oven thermostat, check it with an oven thermometer. Simply set the oven and place the thermometer inside for 20 to 30 minutes. If they do not agree, adjust the oven temperature accordingly. For example, if you set your oven at 350°F and the thermometer reads 340°F, increase the oven setting until thermometer reads 350°F.*

COFFEE CREAM ANGEL CAKE

1 package Duncan Hines Deluxe Angel Food Cake Mix

1⅓ cups water

1 package (4-serving-size) vanilla pudding and pie filling mix

1½ cups milk

1 tablespoon powdered instant coffee

2 cups whipping cream

¼ cup sugar

1 teaspoon vanilla extract

¼ cup chopped nuts

1. Preheat oven to 375°F.

2. Prepare cake with water as directed on package. Pour batter into ungreased 10-inch tube pan. Cut through batter with knife or spatula to remove large air bubbles.

3. Bake at 375°F for 30 to 40 minutes or until top crust is golden brown, firm and looks dry. Do not underbake. To cool, hang pan upside down on funnel or bottle at least 1½ hours.

4. Combine pudding mix, milk and coffee powder in saucepan. Cook pudding as directed on package. Cool to room temperature.

5. Place cake, wider-side-down, on serving plate. Cut around cake 1½ inches from outer edge and 2 inches down into cake. Gently remove center; tear into small pieces. Tightly fill the bottom of the hole with some of the cake pieces. Reserve remaining pieces.

6. Whip cream until stiff; beat in sugar and vanilla extract. Beat pudding smooth; fold two-thirds whipped cream and remaining cake pieces into pudding. Turn coffee cream mixture into cake shell. Sprinkle filling with nuts. Spread remaining whipped cream on sides and top edge of cake. Refrigerate until firm, preferably overnight.

12 to 14 servings

APRICOT SUPREME CAKE

1 package Duncan Hines
Deluxe White Cake Mix
1 cup plus 3 tablespoons
apricot nectar
4 large eggs
½ cup Crisco Oil or Puritan
Oil
1 package (4-serving-size)
vanilla instant pudding
and pie filling mix

6 tablespoons butter or
margarine
½ teaspoon vanilla extract
4 cups confectioners' sugar
1 can (8¾ ounces) apricot
halves, drained
Mint leaves, if desired

1. Preheat oven to 350°F. Grease and flour 10-inch tube pan.

2. Combine dry cake mix, 1 cup apricot nectar, eggs, oil and pudding mix in large mixer bowl. Beat 4 minutes at medium speed. Turn batter into pan and spread evenly.

3. Bake at 350°F for 50 to 55 minutes or until toothpick inserted in center comes out clean. Cool in pans on racks 10 minutes. Remove from pans. Cool completely on racks.

4. For frosting, cream butter and vanilla extract in bowl. Add confectioners' sugar alternately with remaining 3 tablespoons apricot nectar, beating until smooth after each addition. Spread on cooled cake and decorate with apricot halves and mint leaves.

12 to 16 servings

CHOCOLATE CHERRY TORTE

1 package Duncan Hines
   Deluxe Devil's Food Cake
   Mix
3 large eggs
½ cup Crisco Oil or Puritan
   Oil
1⅓ cups water
1 can (17.5 ounces)
   ready-to-serve chocolate
   pudding
5 tablespoons rum
1 cup coarsely chopped
   walnuts

¾ cup red maraschino
   cherries, quartered and
   drained
1 container (4 ounces)
   frozen non-dairy whipped
   topping, thawed
2 ounces (2 squares)
   unsweetened chocolate,
   shaved with paring knife
   or vegetable peeler

1. Preheat oven to 350°F. Grease and flour two 9×9×2-inch pans.

2. Combine dry cake mix, eggs, oil and water in large mixer bowl. Mix cake as directed on package. Divide batter evenly in pans.

3. Bake at 350°F for 25 to 30 minutes or until toothpick inserted in center comes out clean. Cool in pans on racks 10 minutes. Remove from pans; cool completely on racks. Chill cooled layers to make splitting easier.

4. For filling, place pudding in bowl. Blend in 1 tablespoon rum, walnuts and cherries. Fold in whipped topping.

5. Split each cake into 2 thin layers. Place one top layer cut-side-down on serving plate and drizzle with 1 tablespoon rum. Spread one-fourth of filling mixture over layer, almost to edges. Sprinkle with one-fourth of chocolate. Place bottom layer on filling; press lightly. Drizzle cake with one tablespoon rum. Spread evenly with one-fourth of filling and sprinkle with one-fourth chocolate. Place bottom half of remaining layer on stack and drizzle with 1 tablespoon rum. Top with one-fourth filling and one-fourth chocolate. Place remaining layer on cake, cut-side-down. Drizzle with remaining tablespoon rum; spread with remaining filling and top with remaining chocolate. Refrigerate until set.

9 to 12 servings

Chocolate Cherry Torte

GLAZED APRICOT LAYER

1 **package Duncan Hines Deluxe Yellow Cake Mix**
3 **large eggs**
⅓ **cup Crisco Oil or Puritan Oil**

1¼ **cups water**
¾ **cup flaked coconut**
1 **can (16 ounces) apricot halves in syrup**
½ **cup apricot preserves**

1. Preheat oven to 350°F. Grease and flour two 9×1½-inch pans.

2. Combine dry cake mix, eggs, oil and water in large mixer bowl. Mix cake as directed on package. Divide batter evenly in pans. Sprinkle coconut over batter in one pan. Bake and cool as directed on package.

3. Place cooled coconut cake layer on plate. (Wrap and freeze plain layer for later use.)

4. Drain apricots, reserving 1 tablespoon syrup. Arrange apricot halves cut-side-down around edge of cake. Combine apricot preserves and 1 tablespoon reserved syrup in small saucepan. Heat, stirring occasionally, over low heat until the mixture is warm. Spoon mixture over each apricot, allowing it to drizzle down sides of cake. Refrigerate until ready to serve.

8 servings

Easy Cakes for Everyday

BANANA SPLIT CAKES

1 package Duncan Hines
  Deluxe Chocolate Chip
  Cake Mix
3 large eggs
⅓ cup Crisco Oil or Puritan
  Oil
1 cup water

3 medium bananas
  Lemon juice
4 cups whipped topping
1 jar (12 ounces) chocolate
  fudge topping
⅓ cup chopped nuts
15 red maraschino cherries

1. Preheat oven to 350°F. Grease and flour 13×9×2-inch pan.

2. Combine dry cake mix, eggs, oil and water in large mixer bowl. Mix, bake and cool cake as directed on package.

3. To serve, peel and slice bananas. Sprinkle with lemon juice to prevent darkening; set aside.

4. Spread 2 cups of whipped topping over cooled cake. Cut cake into 15 pieces (about 3×2½ inches). Top each piece with several banana slices, a dollop of whipped topping and about 1 tablespoon fudge topping. Sprinkle with chopped nuts and top with maraschino cherry. Refrigerate any leftover cake.

15 servings

DUMP CAKE

1 can (20 ounces) crushed
   pineapple in syrup,
   undrained
1 can (21 ounces) cherry pie
   filling

1 package Duncan Hines
   Deluxe Yellow Cake Mix
1 cup chopped pecans
½ cup (1 stick) butter or
   margarine, cut in thin slices

1. Preheat oven to 350°F. Grease 13×9×2-inch pan.

2. Spoon undrained pineapple into pan; spread evenly. Add pie filling and spread in even layer. Sprinkle dry cake mix onto cherry layer; spread evenly. Sprinkle pecans over cake mix. Place butter over top.

3. Bake at 350°F for 48 to 53 minutes. Serve warm or cooled.

12 to 16 servings

MOCHA CHARMER

1 package Duncan Hines
  Deluxe Swiss Chocolate
  Cake Mix
4 tablespoons powdered
  instant coffee
4 large eggs
½ cup Crisco Oil or Puritan
  Oil
1⅓ cups water
  Blanched almonds

½ ounce (½ square)
  semisweet chocolate,
  melted
¼ cup Crisco shortening
¼ cup unsweetened cocoa
⅛ teaspoon salt
2¼ cups confectioners' sugar
2 tablespoons milk
½ teaspoon vanilla extract

1. Preheat oven to 350°F. Grease and flour 13×9×2-inch pan.

2. Place dry cake mix, 3 tablespoons instant coffee, 3 eggs, oil and water in large mixer bowl. Mix, bake and cool cake as directed on package.

3. Dip top of each almond in melted chocolate. Place on wax paper and refrigerate until chocolate sets.

4. For frosting*, combine shortening, 1 egg, cocoa, 1 tablespoon instant coffee and salt in bowl. Add confectioners' sugar alternately with milk, beating until smooth. Blend in vanilla. Add more confectioners' sugar to thicken or milk to thin frosting as needed. Spread on cooled cake and decorate with chocolate-tipped almonds.

16 servings

Or in medium bowl, dissolve 1 teaspoon instant coffee powder in 1 teaspoon hot water; stir in 1 can Duncan Hines Chocolate Frosting.

GOLDEN CRUNCH CAKE

2 cups fine vanilla wafer crumbs
1 cup finely chopped pecans
½ cup sugar
¼ cup (½ stick) butter or margarine

1 package Duncan Hines Butter Recipe Golden Cake Mix
3 large eggs
½ cup (1 stick) butter or margarine, softened
⅔ cup water

1. Preheat oven to 375°F. Grease two 9×5×3-inch pans.

2. Combine wafer crumbs, pecans and sugar in bowl. Add ¼ cup butter and cut in with pastry blender until crumbs are fine. Divide evenly in pans; press on bottom and sides.

3. Combine dry cake mix, eggs, ½ cup butter and water in large mixer bowl. Mix cake as directed on package. Divide batter evenly in pans.

4. Bake at 375°F for 50 to 60 minutes or until toothpick inserted in center comes out clean. Cool in pans on racks 5 minutes. Carefully loosen cake from pans and turn upside down on racks; cool completely.   *20 servings*

LEMON PEAR UPSIDE-DOWN CAKE

½ cup (1 stick) butter or margarine
1 cup packed brown sugar
1 can (29 ounces) pear halves in syrup
Red maraschino cherry halves

1 package Duncan Hines Deluxe Lemon Cake Mix
3 large eggs
⅓ cup Crisco Oil or Puritan Oil
Sweetened whipped cream

1. Preheat oven to 350°F.

2. Melt butter in 13×9×2-inch pan. Sprinkle brown sugar evenly in pan. Drain pears; reserve syrup. Cut pear halves in quarters. Arrange pears and cherries in pan.

3. Add enough water to reserved pear syrup to make 1¼ cups. Place dry cake mix, liquid, eggs and oil in large mixer bowl. Mix cake as directed on package. Turn into pan and spread evenly over fruit.

4. Bake at 350°F for 45 to 50 minutes or until toothpick inserted in center comes out clean. Let stand for 5 minutes. Invert on large platter. Serve with whipped cream.   *12 to 16 servings*

Golden Crunch Cake

RAISIN-FILLED ORANGE CAKE

1 package Duncan Hines
  Deluxe Orange Cake Mix
3 large eggs
⅓ cup Crisco Oil or Puritan
  Oil
1¼ cups water
2 tablespoons brown sugar
2 tablespoons all-purpose
  flour

1 cup orange juice
¾ cup dark raisins, coarsely
  chopped
1 envelope (1¼ ounces)
  whipped topping mix
¼ cup flaked coconut
½ teaspoon grated orange
  peel

1. Preheat oven to 350°F. Grease and flour two 9×1½-inch round layer pans.

2. Combine dry cake mix, eggs, oil and water in large mixer bowl. Mix, bake and cool cake as directed on package.

3. For filling, combine brown sugar and flour in saucepan. Add orange juice gradually, stirring until smooth. Add raisins. Cook and stir over low heat until mixture boils and thickens, 8 to 10 minutes. Cool.

4. Spread cooled raisin filling between layers. Frost top and sides of cake with prepared whipped topping. Toss coconut with orange peel; sprinkle over top of cake.

12 to 16 servings

CINNAMON RIPPLE CAKE

1 package Duncan Hines
   Deluxe Angel Food Cake
   Mix
1⅓ cups water
3½ teaspoons ground
   cinnamon

¾ cup whipping cream
½ cup cold milk
⅓ cup confectioners' sugar
1 teaspoon vanilla extract

1. Preheat oven to 375°F.

2. Prepare cake with water as directed on package. Spoon one-fourth of batter into ungreased 10-inch tube pan and spread evenly. With small fine sieve, sprinkle one teaspoon cinnamon over batter. Repeat layering two more times, ending with batter.

3. Bake at 375°F for 30 to 40 minutes or until top crust is golden brown, firm and looks very dry. Do not underbake.

4. To cool cake, hang pan upside down on bottle or funnel. When completely cooled, remove from pan.

5. To serve, beat whipping cream and milk in chilled bowl with chilled beaters until thick. Blend in confectioners' sugar, vanilla extract and remaining ½ teaspoon cinnamon. Cut cake into slices and top with cinnamon cream.

12 to 16 servings

EASY GERMAN CHOCOLATE CAKE

1 package Duncan Hines
   Deluxe Swiss Chocolate
   Cake Mix
3 large eggs
½ cup Crisco Oil or Puritan
   Oil
1¼ cups water
1 cup chopped nuts

⅓ cup butter or regular
   margarine, melted
1 cup packed light brown
   sugar
1 can (3½ ounces) flaked
   coconut
¼ cup milk

1. Preheat oven to 350°F. Grease and flour 13×9×2-inch pan.

2. Combine dry cake mix, eggs, oil and water in large mixer bowl. Mix cake as directed on package. Stir in ½ cup nuts. Turn batter into pan and spread evenly.

3. Bake at 350°F for 35 to 40 minutes or until toothpick inserted in center comes out clean. Cool in pan on rack.

4. For topping, combine butter, brown sugar, coconut, milk and remaining ½ cup nuts. Spread evenly over cooled cake. Place under broiler and broil 2 to 3 minutes or until bubbly.

12 to 16 servings

CARROT CAKE SUPREME

1 package Duncan Hines
  Deluxe Carrot Cake Mix
3 large eggs
½ cup Crisco Oil or Puritan
  Oil
½ cup water
½ cup finely chopped nuts
1 can (8 ounces) crushed
  pineapple, undrained

2 packages (3 ounces each)
  cream cheese, softened
⅓ cup butter or margarine,
  softened
1½ teaspoons vanilla extract
3½ cups confectioners' sugar
1 teaspoon milk

1. Preheat oven to 350°F. Grease and flour 13×9×2-inch pan.

2. Combine dry cake mix, eggs, oil, water, nuts and undrained pineapple in large mixer bowl. Mix cake as directed on package. Turn batter into pan and spread evenly.

3. Bake at 350°F for 35 to 40 minutes or until toothpick inserted in center comes out clean. Cool in pan on rack.

4. For cream cheese frosting*, beat cream cheese, butter and vanilla extract in bowl. Add confectioners' sugar and milk; beat until smooth and creamy. Add more confectioners' sugar to thicken or milk to thin as needed. Spread on cooled cake. Refrigerate until ready to serve.

16 to 20 servings

Or in medium size bowl, mix 4 ounces softened cream cheese and 2 teaspoons lemon juice with 1 can Duncan Hines Vanilla Frosting until well blended.

Tip: *Orange and lemon peel make easy decorations for white, lemon or orange frosted cakes. Simply peel long, thin strands of orange or lemon rind with a vegetable peeler and arrange like party streamers on top of cake.*

RHUBARB-SAUCED STRAWBERRY CAKE

1 package Duncan Hines
  Deluxe Strawberry Cake
  Mix
¾ cup water
½ cup orange juice
3 large eggs
⅓ cup Crisco Oil or Puritan
  Oil

6 cups sliced rhubarb
2 cups sugar
½ teaspoon grated orange
  peel
¼ teaspoon ground
  cinnamon
¼ teaspoon ground nutmeg

1. Preheat oven to 350°F. Grease and flour 15½×10½×1-inch jelly-roll pan.

2. Place dry cake mix, water, orange juice, eggs and oil in large mixer bowl. Mix cake as directed on package. Turn batter into pan and spread evenly.

3. Bake at 350°F for 25 to 30 minutes or until toothpick inserted in center comes out clean. Cool in pan on rack.

4. For rhubarb sauce, combine rhubarb, sugar, orange peel, cinnamon and nutmeg in 2-quart saucepan. Cook over high heat until mixture boils; reduce heat to low and simmer, covered, 5 to 7 minutes or until rhubarb is tender; cool. To serve, cut cake into squares and spoon sauce over cake.

15 servings

NEW ORLEANS CRUMB CAKE

1 package Duncan Hines
Deluxe Devil's Food Cake
Mix
3 large eggs
½ cup Crisco Oil or Puritan
Oil
1⅓ cups water
1 cup graham cracker
crumbs

3 tablespoons Crisco
shortening, melted
1 package (6 ounces)
semisweet chocolate
pieces (1 cup)
½ cup chopped nuts
Sweetened whipped
cream, if desired

1. Preheat oven to 350°F. Grease and flour 13×9×2-inch pan.

2. Combine dry cake mix, eggs, oil and water in large mixer bowl. Mix cake as directed on package. Turn batter into pan and spread evenly.

3. Combine graham cracker crumbs and melted shortening; mix well. Stir in chocolate pieces and nuts. Sprinkle evenly over batter.

4. Bake at 350°F for 40 to 50 minutes or until toothpick inserted in center comes out clean. Cool in pan on rack. Serve with whipped cream.

16 servings

PEANUT BUTTER ANGEL ROLL

1 package Duncan Hines Deluxe Angel Food Cake Mix
1⅓ cups water
¼ cup confectioners' sugar
1 cup Jif Peanut Butter
½ cup chopped peanuts
3 tablespoons orange marmalade
3 tablespoons honey
1½ cups confectioners' sugar
2 tablespoons orange juice

1. Preheat oven to 350°F. Line 15½×10½×1-inch jelly-roll pan with foil allowing foil to extend 1 inch above rim of pan.

2. Prepare cake with water as directed on package. Turn batter into foil-lined pan and spread evenly. Cut through batter with knife or spatula to remove large air bubbles.

3. Bake at 350°F for 30 minutes or until top springs back when lightly touched with fingertip. At once turn cake out onto towel covered with ¼ cup confectioners' sugar. Gently peel off foil. Roll up cake, starting at narrow end, rolling up towel with cake. Cool on rack.

4. For filling, combine peanut butter, peanuts, orange marmalade and honey; mix well. Unroll cake and spread entire surface with filling; reroll.

5. For glaze, combine 1½ cups confectioners' sugar and orange juice. Beat until smooth. Drizzle glaze over cake.

12 to 16 servings

CHERRY NUT CAKE

1 package Duncan Hines
  Deluxe Cherry Cake Mix
1 package (4-serving-size)
  vanilla instant pudding
  and pie filling mix
1¼ cups buttermilk

4 large eggs
½ cup Crisco Oil or Puritan
  Oil
1 cup flaked coconut
1 cup finely chopped pecans
  Confectioners' sugar

1. Preheat oven to 350°F. Grease and flour 10-inch fluted tube pan.

2. Combine dry cake mix, instant pudding mix, buttermilk, eggs and oil in large mixer bowl. Mix cake as directed on package. Stir in coconut and pecans. Turn batter into pan and spread evenly.

3. Bake at 350°F for 50 to 60 minutes or until toothpick inserted in center comes out clean. Cool in pan on rack 1 hour. Remove cake from pan and let stand overnight before serving.

4. To serve, sift confectioners' sugar over top of cake.

12 to 16 servings

SOCK-IT-TO-ME CAKE

1 package Duncan Hines
Butter Recipe Golden
Cake Mix
1 cup finely chopped pecans
2 tablespoons brown sugar
2 teaspoons ground
cinnamon
1 cup dairy sour cream

⅓ cup Crisco Oil or Puritan
Oil
¼ cup sugar
¼ cup water
4 large eggs
1 cup confectioners' sugar
2 tablespoons milk

1. Preheat oven to 375°F. Grease and flour 10-inch tube pan.

2. For filling, combine 2 tablespoons cake mix, pecans, brown sugar and cinnamon; mix well. Set aside.

3. Combine remaining dry cake mix, sour cream, oil, sugar, water and eggs in large mixer bowl. Beat 2 minutes at high speed. Turn two-thirds of batter into pan; sprinkle with filling. Spoon remaining batter evenly over filling mixture.

4. Bake at 375°F for 45 to 55 minutes or until toothpick inserted in center comes out clean. Cool in pan on rack 25 minutes; remove from pan.

5. For glaze*, blend together confectioners' sugar and milk; drizzle over warm cake.

12 to 16 servings

*Or heat ⅔ cup Duncan Hines Vanilla Frosting in small saucepan over medium heat, stirring constantly, until thin.

FRENCH APPLE CAKE

3 **cooking apples, pared, cored and sliced (about 3 cups)**

⅔ **cup sugar**

1 **tablespoon all-purpose flour**

½ **teaspoon ground cinnamon**

2 **tablespoons butter or margarine, melted**

2 **tablespoons lemon juice**

1 **package Duncan Hines Deluxe White Cake Mix**

3 **large eggs**

⅓ **cup Crisco Oil or Puritan Oil**

1¼ **cups water**

1. Preheat oven to 350°F. Grease 13×9×2-inch pan.

2. Arrange apples in pan. Mix sugar, flour and cinnamon; sprinkle over apples. Combine melted butter and lemon juice; drizzle over apples.

3. Place dry cake mix, eggs, oil and water in large mixer bowl. Mix cake as directed on package. Turn batter into pan over apples and spread evenly.

4. Bake at 350°F for 40 to 50 minutes or until toothpick inserted in center comes out clean. Cool 1 to 2 minutes in pan. Invert on large platter or tray; remove pan after 1 to 2 minutes. Serve warm.

12 to 16 servings

Easy Cakes for Everyday   37

ORANGE CINNAMON TEA CAKE

1   package Duncan Hines
    Deluxe Orange Cake Mix
3   large eggs
⅓   cup Crisco Oil or Puritan
    Oil
1¼ cups water

½   cup plus ⅓ cup chopped
    walnuts
⅓   cup orange juice
⅓   cup sugar
1   teaspoon ground
    cinnamon

1. Preheat oven to 350°F. Grease and flour 10-inch tube pan.

2. Combine dry cake mix, eggs, oil and water in large mixer bowl. Mix cake as directed on package; stir in ½ cup chopped walnuts. Turn batter into pan and spread evenly.

3. Bake at 350°F for 45 to 55 minutes or until toothpick inserted in center comes out clean. Cool in pan on rack 25 minutes, then remove from pan.

4. Pour orange juice over warm cake and immediately sprinkle with mixture of sugar, cinnamon and remaining ⅓ cup chopped walnuts.

16 servings

TOASTY TOPPED CAKE SLICES

1 package Duncan Hines
Deluxe Yellow Cake Mix
3 large eggs
⅓ cup Crisco Oil or Puritan
Oil
1¼ cups water

2 medium bananas
2 cups miniature
marshmallows
1 package (6 ounces)
semisweet chocolate
pieces (1 cup)

1. Preheat oven to 350°F. Grease and flour two 8½×4½×2½-inch loaf pans.

2. Combine dry cake mix, eggs, oil and water in large mixer bowl. Mix cake as directed on package. Divide batter evenly in pans.

3. Bake at 350°F for 40 to 45 minutes or until toothpick inserted in center comes out clean. Cool in pans on racks 10 minutes. Remove from pans; cool completely on racks.

4. Slice each loaf into 8 to 10 slices. Place, cut-side-down, on large baking sheet. Peel and slice bananas; arrange on cake slices. Top with marshmallows and chocolate pieces. Place in 350°F oven 12 to 15 minutes or until chocolate melts.

16 to 20 servings

Note. Slices may be wrapped in foil and heated over campfire instead of in oven.

CHOCOLATE ZUCCHINI CAKE

1 package Duncan Hines
  Deluxe Deep Chocolate
  Cake Mix
1 teaspoon ground
  cinnamon
3 large eggs
½ cup Crisco Oil or Puritan
  Oil
1¼ cups water

1 cup shredded, unpared
  zucchini
2 packages (3 ounces each)
  cream cheese, softened
⅓ cup butter or margarine,
  softened
1½ teaspoons vanilla extract
3½ cups confectioners' sugar
1 teaspoon milk
¼ cup chopped nuts

1. Preheat oven to 350°F. Grease and flour 10-inch tube pan.

2. Combine dry cake mix and cinnamon in large mixer bowl. Add eggs, oil and water; blend, then beat 2 minutes at medium speed; fold in zucchini. Turn batter into pan and spread evenly.

3. Bake at 350°F for 50 to 60 minutes or until toothpick inserted in center comes out clean. Cool in pan on rack 25 minutes. Remove from pan; cool completely on rack.

4. For frosting*, beat cream cheese, butter, and vanilla in bowl. Add confectioners' sugar and milk; mix until creamy. Add confectioners' sugar to thicken or milk to thin as needed. Spread on cooled cake. Sprinkle with nuts. Refrigerate until ready to serve.

12 to 16 servings

Or in medium size bowl, mix 4 ounces softened cream cheese and 2 teaspoons lemon juice with 1 can Duncan Hines Vanilla Frosting until well blended.

NUTTY CRUNCH CAKE

1 package Duncan Hines
  Deluxe Carrot Cake Mix
4 large eggs
⅓ cup Crisco Oil or Puritan
  Oil
¾ cup water
⅓ cup all-purpose flour

¼ cup sugar
½ cup plus 1 tablespoon Jif
  Extra Crunchy Peanut
  Butter
½ cup confectioners' sugar
1 tablespoon milk
½ teaspoon vanilla extract

1. Preheat oven to 325°F. Grease and flour 8½- or 10-inch fluted tube pan.

2. Combine dry cake mix, eggs, oil and water in large mixer bowl. Mix cake as directed on package. Turn half of batter into pan and spread evenly.

3. For filling, combine flour and sugar in small bowl. Cut in ½ cup peanut butter with pastry blender until crumbly. Sprinkle filling over batter in pan. Spread remaining batter over filling.

4. Bake at 325°F for 50 to 55 minutes or until toothpick inserted in center comes out clean. Cool in pan on rack 25 minutes. Remove from pan; cool completely on rack.

5. For glaze, combine confectioners' sugar, milk, 1 tablespoon peanut butter and vanilla in small mixer bowl. Beat until smooth. Drizzle glaze over cooled cake.   *12 to 16 servings*

Children's Party Cakes

MISTER FUNNY FACE

1 package Duncan Hines
   Deluxe White Cake Mix
3 large egg whites or 3 large,
   whole eggs
⅓ cup Crisco Oil or Puritan
   Oil
1¼ cups water
½ gallon vanilla ice cream

Whole pecans
Dark raisins
Red hots
1 quart fresh strawberries,
   halved or 2 packages (10
   ounces each) frozen
   strawberry halves, thawed

1. Preheat oven to 350°F. Line 24 muffin cups with paper baking cups or grease and flour muffin cups.

2. Combine dry cake mix, egg whites, oil and water in large mixer bowl. Mix cake as directed on package. Spoon batter into muffin cups, filling half full.

3. Bake at 350°F for 15 to 20 minutes or until toothpick inserted in center comes out clean. Cool for 15 minutes. (Remove liners if used.)

4. To serve, turn each cupcake upside down on dessert plate. Place one scoop ice cream on top. Decorate ice cream as face, using whole pecans for ears, raisins for eyes and red hots for mouth. Spoon strawberries around bottom of cupcake; place one strawberry half on top as hat.

24 servings

TEDDY BEAR CAKE

1 package Duncan Hines
Deluxe Cake Mix (any
flavor)
3 large eggs
Crisco Oil or Puritan Oil
Water
1 can (16 ounces) chocolate
syrup
1⅓ cups Jif Creamy Peanut
Butter

3 tablespoons light corn
syrup
2 cups confectioners' sugar
½ cup Crisco shortening
2 tablespoons water
¼ teaspoon vanilla extract
Licorice strings
Gumdrops

1. Preheat oven to 350°F. Grease and flour one 10×2-inch round layer pan and 5 muffin cups.

2. Combine dry cake mix, eggs and the amount of oil and water listed on package in large mixer bowl. Mix as directed on package. Fill muffin cups one-half full with batter; turn remaining batter into round pan and spread evenly.

3. Bake at 350°F for 12 to 15 minutes for cupcakes and 50 to 55 minutes for round cake or until toothpicks inserted in centers come out clean. Cool in pans on racks 10 minutes. Remove from pans; cool completely on racks.

4. For chocolate-peanut frosting, combine chocolate syrup, peanut butter and corn syrup; mix well. For white frosting, combine confectioners' sugar, shortening, water and vanilla extract in bowl; beat until smooth and of spreading consistency.

5. Spread chocolate frosting on cooled round cake and two cupcakes for ears. Position ears at top of cake. Place remaining cupcakes on lower portion for snout (see photo). Spread white frosting on snout and ear and eye areas. Use licorice and gumdrops for face.

12 to 16 servings

ICE CREAM CONE CAKES

1 package Duncan Hines
  Deluxe Cake Mix (any
  flavor)
3 large eggs
  Crisco Oil or Puritan Oil
  Water
1 package (6 ounces)
  semisweet chocolate
  pieces

5 cups confectioners' sugar
¾ cup Crisco shortening
⅓ cup non-dairy creamer
½ cup water
2 teaspoons vanilla extract
½ teaspoon salt
  Chocolate jimmies
  Red maraschino cherries
  with stems

1. Preheat oven to 350°F. Grease and flour one 8×1½-inch round layer pan and one 8×8×2-inch pan.

2. Combine dry cake mix, eggs and the amount of oil and water listed on package in large mixer bowl. Mix cake as directed on package. Turn about 2 cups batter into round pan and about 3 cups batter into square pan; spread evenly. (Batter should be ¾-inch deep.)

3. Bake at 350°F for 30 to 35 minutes or until toothpick inserted in center comes out clean. Cool in pans on racks 10 minutes. Remove from pans; cool completely on racks.

4. For frosting, melt chocolate in saucepan over low heat; set aside. Combine confectioners' sugar, shortening, non-dairy creamer, water and vanilla in large mixer bowl. Beat at medium speed 3 minutes, then at high speed 5 minutes. Add more confectioners' sugar to thicken or more water to thin frosting as needed. Divide frosting in half. Blend melted chocolate into one half.

5. Cut cooled cake and arrange as shown. Spread some of the chocolate frosting on cone parts. Decorate with remaining chocolate frosting, using decorator bag and writing tip (see photo). Spread white frosting on ice cream part of cake. Sprinkle chocolate jimmies over cones and decorate ice cream part with cherries.

12 to 16 servings

  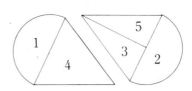

BACK-TO-SCHOOL PENCIL CAKE

1 package Duncan Hines
   Deluxe Cake Mix (any
   flavor)
3 large eggs
   Crisco Oil or Puritan Oil
   Water
5 cups sifted confectioners'
   sugar

¾ cup Crisco shortening
⅓ cup non-dairy creamer
½ cup water
2 teaspoons vanilla extract
½ teaspoon salt
   Food coloring (red and
   yellow)
   Chocolate jimmies

1. Preheat oven to 350°F. Grease and flour 13×9×2-inch pan.

2. Combine dry cake mix, eggs and amount of oil and water listed on package in large mixer bowl. Mix, bake and cool cake as directed on package.

3. For frosting, combine confectioners' sugar, shortening, non-dairy creamer, water, vanilla and salt in large mixer bowl. Beat 3 minutes at medium speed. Increase to high speed and beat 5 minutes more. Add more confectioners' sugar to thicken or water to thin frosting as needed. Measure a small amount of frosting and tint pink with red food coloring. Color remaining frosting with yellow food coloring.

4. Cut cooled cake and arrange as shown. Spread pink frosting on cake for eraser at one end and for wood at the other end. Spread yellow frosting over remaining cake. Decorate with chocolate jimmies for pencil tip and eraser band.

12 to 16 servings

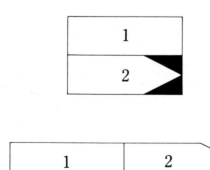

Back-To-School Pencil Cake

HOPSCOTCH CAKE

1 package Duncan Hines Deluxe Yellow Cake Mix
3 large eggs
⅓ cup Crisco Oil or Puritan Oil
1¼ cups water

1 package (6 ounces) butterscotch-flavored pieces (1 cup)
3 tablespoons butter or margarine
3½ cups confectioners' sugar
4-5 tablespoons milk
8 licorice sticks

1. Preheat oven to 350°F. Grease and flour 13×9×2-inch baking pan.

2. Combine dry cake mix, eggs, oil and water in large mixer bowl. Mix, bake and cool cake, as directed on package.

3. Combine butterscotch pieces and butter in small saucepan. Melt over low heat, stirring constantly. Combine butterscotch mixture and confectioners' sugar in bowl. Add milk gradually, beating until mixture is of spreading consistency. Spread on cooled cake. Decorate top with licorice sticks to make hopscotch pattern. Sketch numbers in squares.

20 to 24 servings

BIRTHDAY CAKELETS

2 packages Duncan Hines
   Deluxe Devil's Food Cake
   Mix
6 large eggs
1 cup Crisco Oil or Puritan
   Oil
2⅔ cups water

2 cups light corn syrup
4 large egg whites
⅛ teaspoon salt
   Red food coloring
½ teaspoon peppermint
   extract

1. Preheat oven to 350°F. Grease and flour two 13×9×2-inch pans.

2. Combine dry cake mix, whole eggs, oil and water in large mixer bowl. Mix, bake and cool cakes as directed on package. Freeze cooled cakes at least 2 hours.

3. For frosting, heat syrup to boiling. Beat egg whites in large mixer bowl at medium speed until frothy. Add salt and continue beating until soft peaks form. Turn mixer to high speed and gradually add hot corn syrup, beating until soft peaks form. Fold in food coloring to tint delicate pink. Fold in peppermint extract.

4. Draw heart on 3-inch square of cardboard; cut out. Set heart pattern on lower left corner of one cake. Cut around pattern through cake. Cut out 11 more hearts before removing cake pieces. Repeat with remaining cake.

5. Frost sides and tops of each cake heart. Insert pink birthday candle in center of each heart.

24 servings

Tip: *Before frosting cakes, brush off any loose crumbs, which will mix in with the frosting. If necessary, apply a thin coating of frosting first to seal in any remaining crumbs.*

FUDGE 'N' BANANA CUPCAKES

1 package Duncan Hines
Deluxe Devil's Food Cake
Mix
3 large eggs
½ cup Crisco Oil or Puritan
Oil
1⅓ cups water
½ cup (1 stick) butter or
margarine

2 ounces (2 squares)
unsweetened chocolate
1 pound confectioners'
sugar
½ cup half-and-half
1 teaspoon vanilla extract
4 medium bananas
2 tablespoons lemon juice

1. Preheat oven to 350°F. Line 24 muffin cups with paper baking cups.

2. Combine dry cake mix, eggs, oil and water in large mixer bowl. Mix, bake and cool cupcakes as directed on package.

3. For frosting*, melt butter and chocolate in heavy saucepan over low heat. Remove from heat. Add confectioners' sugar alternately with half-and-half, mixing until smooth after each addition. Beat in vanilla extract. Add more confectioners' sugar to thicken or milk to thin as needed.

4. Using small paring knife, remove cone-shaped piece from top center of each cupcake. Dot top of each cone with frosting. Frost top of each cupcake spreading frosting down into cone-shaped hole. Slice bananas and dip in lemon juice. Stand three banana slices in each hole. Set cone-shaped pieces, pointed-side-up, on banana slices.   *24 cupcakes*

Or use 1 can Duncan Hines Dark Dutch Fudge or Chocolate Frosting.

CUPCAKE CONES

1 package Duncan Hines Deluxe Devil's Food Cake Mix	1⅓ cups water
3 large eggs	24 flat-bottom ice cream cones
½ cup Crisco Oil or Puritan Oil	Ice cream

1. Preheat oven to 350°F. Set ice cream cones in muffin pans with small cups.

2. Combine dry cake mix, eggs, oil and water in large mixer bowl. Mix cake as directed on package. Spoon 2 tablespoons batter into each cone.

3. Bake at 350°F for 20 to 25 minutes or until toothpick inserted in center comes out clean. Cool on racks.

4. To serve, top each cone with a scoop of ice cream.

24 servings

Holiday Baking

PINEAPPLE CHRISTMAS TREE CAKE

½ cup (1 stick) butter or margarine, melted
1 cup packed brown sugar
1 can (20 ounces) pineapple chunks, drained
  Red and green maraschino cherries (about 5 each), cut into quarters

1 package Duncan Hines Deluxe Pineapple Cake Mix
3 large eggs
⅓ cup Crisco Oil or Puritan Oil
1¼ cups water
  Sweetened whipped cream, if desired

1. Preheat oven to 350°F.

2. Place melted butter in 13×9×2-inch baking pan. Sprinkle brown sugar evenly in pan. Arrange pineapple chunks in pan to form Christmas tree. Start with one chunk in first row, 2 in second, etc. (see photo). Use 4 chunks to make trunk. Place cherry quarters between pineapple chunks to decorate tree.

3. Combine dry cake mix, eggs, oil and water in large mixer bowl. Mix cake as directed on package. Pour batter over fruit in pan and spread evenly.

4. Bake at 350°F for 48 to 53 minutes or until toothpick inserted in center comes out clean. Let stand 5 minutes; turn upside down onto large platter or cookie sheet. Serve warm with sweetened whipped cream.

12 to 16 servings

CHOCOLATE FRUIT CAKE

1⅓ cups chopped pitted dates
1¼ cups sliced candied cherries
1 cup raisins
½ cup chopped candied citron
½ cup chopped candied pineapple
1 cup chopped walnuts
1 cup chopped pecans
½ cup all-purpose flour
1 package Duncan Hines Deluxe Devil's Food Cake Mix
⅔ cup water
½ cup sherry
3 large eggs
½ cup Crisco Oil or Puritan Oil

1. Preheat oven to 275°F. Grease and flour two 9×5×3-inch loaf pans.

2. Combine fruit, nuts and flour in large bowl; toss until fruit is coated with flour.

3. Combine dry cake mix, water, sherry, eggs and oil in large mixer bowl. Mix cake as directed on package. Stir in fruit and nuts. Turn batter into pans and spread evenly.

4. Bake at 275°F for 3 hours or until toothpick inserted in center comes out clean. Cool in pans 20 minutes. Remove from pans; cool completely on racks.

Two 9×5×3-inch loaf cakes

Note: Cakes may be made 1 week ahead. Wrap tightly in foil.

THANKSGIVING CRANBERRY COBBLER

1 package Duncan Hines Deluxe Yellow Cake Mix
½ teaspoon ground cinnamon
¼ teaspoon ground nutmeg
1 cup (2 sticks) butter or margarine, softened
½ cup chopped nuts
1 can (21 ounces) peach pie filling
1 can (16 ounces) whole cranberry sauce
Vanilla ice cream or sweetened whipped cream

1. Preheat oven to 350°F.

2. Combine dry cake mix, cinnamon and nutmeg in bowl. Cut in butter with pastry blender or two knives until crumbly. Stir in nuts; set aside.

3. Combine peach pie filling and cranberry sauce in ungreased 13×9×2-inch pan; mix well. Sprinkle crumb mixture over fruit.

4. Bake at 350°F for 45 to 50 minutes or until golden brown. Serve warm with ice cream or whipped cream.

16 servings

GINGERBREAD PEOPLE

1 package Duncan Hines
Deluxe Spice Cake Mix
2 teaspoons ground ginger
2 large eggs

⅓ cup Crisco Oil or Puritan
Oil
⅓ cup dark molasses
½ cup all-purpose flour
Dark raisins

1. Combine all ingredients, except raisins, in large bowl; mix well (mixture will be soft). Refrigerate 2 hours.

2. Preheat oven to 375°F. Roll dough to ¼-inch thickness on lightly floured surface. Cut with 6-inch cookie cutter. Place on ungreased cookie sheets. Press raisins in dough for eyes and buttons.

3. Bake at 375°F for 8 to 10 minutes or until edges just start to brown. Cool several minutes on cookie sheet, then remove to racks to finish cooling. *About 14 six-inch cookies*

HOLIDAY COFFEE CAKE

1 package Duncan Hines
Butter Recipe Golden
Cake Mix
3 large eggs
½ cup (1 stick) butter or
margarine, softened
⅔ cup water
1½ cups finely chopped
walnuts

½ cup sugar
1 teaspoon ground
cinnamon
2 tablespoons butter or
margarine, melted
1 cup chopped candied
cherries and pineapple

1. Preheat oven to 375°F. Grease and flour 13×9×2-inch pan.

2. Combine dry cake mix, eggs, ½ cup soft butter and water in large mixer bowl. Mix cake as directed on package. Turn into pan and spread evenly.

3. Bake at 375°F for 15 minutes.

4. While cake is baking, mix together walnuts, sugar, cinnamon and 2 tablespoons melted butter. Distribute fruit over partially baked cake. Sprinkle with nut mixture.

5. Bake 35 minutes more or until toothpick inserted in center comes out clean. Cool slightly; cut into squares. Cool completely in pan on rack. *12 to 16 servings*

Gingerbread People

COCONUT CRISPS

1 package Duncan Hines
  Deluxe Yellow Cake Mix
½ cup Crisco Oil or Puritan
  Oil
¼ cup water
1 teaspoon almond extract

1 large egg
1 can (3½ ounces) flaked
  coconut
  Whole unblanched
  almonds or red
  maraschino cherries

1. Preheat oven to 350°F.

2. Combine dry cake mix, oil, water, almond extract and egg in bowl; mix well. Stir in coconut. Drop from teaspoon on ungreased baking sheets. Press whole almond or piece of maraschino cherry in center of each cookie.

3. Bake at 350°F for 10 to 12 minutes or until light golden brown. Cool several minutes on cookie sheet, then remove to racks to finish cooling.

About 6 dozen 2¼-inch cookies

JELLY JEWELS

1 package Duncan Hines
  Deluxe Yellow Cake Mix
¾ cup Crisco shortening
2 large egg yolks
1 tablespoon milk

2 large egg whites
2 tablespoons water
1¼ cups ground nuts
  Red or green jelly

1. Preheat oven to 375°F. Grease cookie sheets.

2. Combine dry cake mix, shortening, egg yolks and milk; mix well. Shape into 1-inch balls.

3. Combine egg whites and water. Beat with fork until blended. Dip balls in egg white mixture, then roll in nuts. Place 2 inches apart on cookie sheets.

4. Bake at 375°F for 12 to 15 minutes or until golden brown. Immediately press thumb or thimble into center of each cookie making a depression. Cool several minutes on cookie sheets, then remove to racks to finish cooling. Before serving, fill depressions with jelly.

About 4 dozen 2-inch cookies

Coconut Crisps (top), Jelly Jewels (bottom)

CHRISTMAS FRUIT BARS

1 package Duncan Hines Deluxe Yellow Cake Mix	1 cup chopped candied mixed fruit
1 large egg	½ cup chopped nuts
¼ cup Crisco Oil or Puritan Oil	1 cup confectioners' sugar
⅓ cup water	2 tablespoons milk
	1 teaspoon lemon juice

1. Preheat oven to 375°F. Grease 13×9×2-inch pan.

2. Empty about half of the dry cake mix into bowl. Add egg, oil and water; mix thoroughly by hand or with mixer at low speed. Blend in remaining cake mix (batter will be thick). Stir in candied fruit and nuts. Turn batter into pan and spread evenly.

3. Bake at 375°F for 25 to 30 minutes or until toothpick inserted in center comes out clean. (Bars will appear slightly puffed and will flatten some when removed from oven.) Set pan on rack.

4. For glaze*, mix confectioners' sugar, milk and lemon juice until smooth. Spread over warm layer. Cut into bars.

About 4 dozen bars

Or heat ⅔ cup Duncan Hines Vanilla Frosting in small saucepan over medium heat, stirring constantly, until thin.

HOLIDAY FRUIT CAKE

1 pound diced mixed
   candied fruit
8 ounces candied cherries,
   chopped
4 ounces candied pineapple,
   chopped
1½ cups finely chopped nuts
1 cup raisins
½ cup all-purpose flour
1 package Duncan Hines
   Deluxe Spice Cake Mix

3 large eggs
½ cup Crisco Oil or Puritan
   Oil
¼ cup water
1 package (4-serving-size)
   vanilla instant pudding
   and pie filling mix
Light corn syrup
Candied pineapple slices
Pecan halves

1. Preheat oven to 300°F. Grease one 10-inch tube pan or two 9×5×3-inch loaf pans. Line with heavy paper or aluminum foil.

2. Combine candied fruit, cherries, 4 oz. pineapple, chopped nuts, raisins and flour in bowl; toss until fruit is coated with flour. Set aside.

3. Place dry cake mix, eggs, oil, water and pudding mix in large mixer bowl. Beat 3 minutes at medium speed (batter will be stiff). Stir in candied fruit mixture. Turn batter into pan or pans; spread evenly.

4. Bake at 300°F for 2 hours for tube pan, 1½ hours for loaf pans; cake is done if toothpick inserted in center comes out clean. Cool completely in pans on racks. Remove cake from pans.

5. Heat corn syrup in small saucepan; brush over cake. Decorate with sliced pineapple and pecan halves. To store, wrap in aluminum foil or plastic wrap, or store in airtight container.

Two 9×5×3-inch loaf cakes or one 10-inch tube cake

Desserts

PEACH CARROT CHEESECAKE

1 package Duncan Hines
Deluxe Carrot Cake Mix
½ cup Crisco Oil or Puritan
Oil
2 cans (16 ounces each)
peach halves in juice
1 envelope unflavored
gelatin
2 packages (8 ounces each)
cream cheese, softened

1 can (14 ounces)
sweetened condensed milk
2 tablespoons lemon juice
1 container (4 ounces)
frozen non-dairy whipped
topping, thawed
1 teaspoon cornstarch
Mint leaves

1. Preheat oven to 350°F. Grease 10-inch springform pan.

2. For crust, combine dry cake mix and oil in bowl; mix well. Turn into pan and spread evenly. Bake at 350°F for 20 minutes. Cool, then refrigerate.

3. For filling, drain peaches reserving 1 cup juice. Combine ½ cup of peach juice and gelatin in saucepan. Cook over low heat, stirring constantly until gelatin dissolves. Reserve 3 peach halves for garnish. Purée remaining peaches in blender until smooth. Combine peaches and gelatin mixture; set aside.

4. Beat cream cheese until smooth in large bowl. Add sweetened condensed milk and lemon juice; mix well. Stir in peach gelatin mixture. Fold in whipped topping. Turn into crust-lined pan and spread evenly.

5. To decorate, slice reserved peaches and arrange in 2-piece clusters on top of cheesecake. For glaze, blend remaining ½ cup peach juice and cornstarch in saucepan. Cook and stir until mixture boils and thickens. Cool. Spoon cooled glaze evenly over cheesecake. Add mint leaves to peach clusters. Refrigerate at least 3 hours before serving.

12 servings

CHOCOLATE REFRIGERATOR DESSERT

1 package Duncan Hines
  Deluxe Swiss Chocolate
  Cake Mix
3 large eggs
½ cup Crisco Oil or Puritan
  Oil
1¼ cups water
1½ cups semisweet chocolate
  pieces

3 large eggs, separated
2 tablespoons sugar
3 cups whipped topping
  Whipped topping for
  garnish
  Red maraschino cherries,
  if desired

1. Preheat oven to 350°F. Grease and flour 10-inch tube pan.

2. Combine dry cake mix, 3 eggs, oil and water in large mixer bowl. Mix, bake and cool cake as directed on package.

3. Melt chocolate in double boiler over hot, not boiling, water. Beat 3 egg yolks with fork. Stir egg yolks and sugar into melted chocolate.

4. Beat 3 egg whites until stiff, not dry, peaks form. Fold beaten egg whites and 3 cups whipped topping into chocolate mixture.

5. Tear cooled cake into small pieces. Place one-third of cake pieces in bottom of 10-inch springform pan. Spoon one-third chocolate mixture over cake pieces. Repeat layers two more times. Refrigerate 24 hours.

6. To serve, unmold and place on serving plate. Decorate with additional whipped topping and garnish with cherries.

12 servings

SWEDISH APPLE CAKE

1 cup packed brown sugar	1 can (20 ounces) apple pie filling
2 tablespoons all-purpose flour	1 package Duncan Hines Deluxe Lemon Cake Mix
¼ teaspoon ground nutmeg	3 large eggs
⅛ teaspoon salt	⅓ cup Crisco Oil or Puritan Oil
1 cup water	1¼ cups water
2 tablespoons butter or margarine	

1. Combine brown sugar, flour, nutmeg and salt in small baking dish. Gradually stir in 1 cup water. Add butter; set aside.

2. Spread apple pie filling in 13×9×2-inch pan.

3. Combine dry cake mix, eggs, oil and 1¼ cups water in large mixer bowl. Mix as directed on package. Spread batter evenly over apples.

4. Place cake and sauce in preheated oven. Bake at 350°F for 43 to 48 minutes or until toothpick inserted in center comes out clean.

5. To serve, spoon warm cake and apples in serving bowls and top with sauce.

16 to 20 servings

CHOCOLATE CRUMB PIE

1 package Duncan Hines
  Deluxe Fudge Marble
  Cake Mix
⅔ cup all-purpose flour
½ teaspoon salt
1 large egg

3 tablespoons Crisco Oil or
  Puritan Oil
2 packages (4-serving-size)
  instant or regular
  chocolate pudding and pie
  filling mix
3½ cups milk

1. Preheat oven to 350°F.

2. For crust, combine dry cake mix (do not add contents of small packet), flour, salt, egg and 2 tablespoons oil in large bowl. Mix until crumbs are deeper, even color and uniformly fine (like graham cracker crumbs). Measure 1½ cups of crumb mixture into each of two 9-inch pie plates. Press firmly against sides and then bottom to make crusts; reserve remaining crumb mixture.

3. Prepare pudding mix with milk as directed on package for pie except add half of reserved small packet to each package of pudding mix before mixing or cooking. Pour into crusts. Mix remaining 1 tablespoon oil with reserved crumbs; sprinkle.

4. Bake at 350°F for 20 to 25 minutes or until golden brown. Cool 1 hour, then refrigerate until serving.   *12 to 16 servings*

CHERRY CAKE COBBLER

1 package Duncan Hines
 Deluxe White Cake Mix
3 large eggs
⅓ cup Crisco Oil or Puritan
 Oil
1¼ cups water
1 cup sugar
2 tablespoons cornstarch

2 cans (16 ounces each)
 pitted red tart cherries
 (undrained)
2 tablespoons butter or
 margarine, melted
1 teaspoon red food coloring
¾ teaspoon almond extract
 Sweetened whipped
 cream or vanilla ice cream

1. Preheat oven to 350°F. Grease and flour 13×9×2-inch pan.

2. Place dry cake mix, eggs, oil and water in large mixer bowl. Mix as directed on package. Turn into pan and spread evenly.

3. Combine sugar and cornstarch in bowl. Add cherries, butter, food coloring and almond extract; mix well. Spoon evenly over batter.

4. Bake at 350°F for 50 to 60 minutes or until golden. Serve warm or cold with whipped cream or ice cream.   *16 servings*

CHOCOLATE SWIRL CHEESECAKE

1 package Duncan Hines
   Deluxe Devil's Food Cake
   Mix
½ cup Crisco Oil or Puritan
   Oil
2 envelopes unflavored
   gelatin
½ cup cold water
⅓ cup all-purpose flour
¾ cup sugar
½ cup milk

4 large eggs, separated
1 package (6 ounces)
   semisweet chocolate
   pieces (1 cup)
⅓ cup whipping cream
2 cups creamed cottage
   cheese
1 teaspoon vanilla extract
½ teaspoon almond extract
1⅓ cups whipped topping

1. Preheat oven to 350°F. Grease 9- or 10-inch springform pan.

2. For crust, combine dry cake mix and oil in bowl; mix well. Turn mixture into pan; press firmly and evenly over bottom.

3. Bake at 350°F for 20 to 25 minutes. Cool on rack.

4. Sprinkle gelatin over cold water to soften. Blend flour and ¼ cup sugar in saucepan. Stir in milk. Cook and stir over medium heat until mixture boils and thickens. Remove from heat. Beat egg yolks with fork; stir a small amount of hot mixture into yolks. Return yolk mixture to saucepan.

5. Cook 1 minute, stirring constantly. Remove from heat. Add softened gelatin; stir until dissolved. Cool to lukewarm.

6. Combine chocolate pieces and whipping cream in heavy saucepan. Heat, stirring constantly, over low heat until chocolate is melted. Cool to lukewarm. Beat cottage cheese 5 minutes at high speed in mixer bowl. Beat in vanilla extract, almond extract and gelatin mixture.

7. Beat egg whites until frothy in mixer bowl. Continue beating, gradually adding ½ cup sugar until stiff peaks form. Fold beaten egg whites into gelatin mixture. Then fold in whipped topping. Spoon one-third filling onto crust, drizzle with chocolate mixture and swirl with spoon, making marble pattern. Repeat with remaining filling and chocolate two more times. Refrigerate 6 hours before serving.

12 to 16 serving

Chocolate Swirl Cheesecake

CHERRY FRUIT 'N' CREAM SQUARES

1 package Duncan Hines
  Deluxe Yellow Cake Mix
½ teaspoon salt
¼ teaspoon baking soda
¾ cup plus 2 tablespoons
  Crisco Oil or Puritan Oil
1 package (8 ounces) cream
  cheese, softened

1 cup confectioners' sugar
1 cup whipped topping
1 can (21 ounces) cherry pie
  filling
  Whipped topping, if
  desired

1. Preheat oven to 350°F.

2. For crust, combine dry cake mix, salt, baking soda and oil. Spread in ungreased 13×9×2-inch pan.

3. Bake at 350°F for 20 minutes or until light brown. Cool.

4. For cream layer, combine cream cheese, confectioners' sugar and whipped topping; mix well. Spread over cooled crust. Carefully spread cherry pie filling over cream layer. Refrigerate at least 1 hour before serving. Decorate with whipped topping, if desired. Store in refrigerator.

16 to 20 servings

FONDUE PARTY

1 package Duncan Hines
  Deluxe Cake Mix (any
  flavor)
3 large eggs
  Crisco Oil or Puritan Oil
  Water
1 package (14 ounces)
  vanilla caramels

2 ounces (2 squares)
  semisweet chocolate
⅔ cup milk
1 tablespoon corn syrup
  Marshmallows
  Strawberries
  Red maraschino cherries

1. One day before serving, preheat oven to 350°F. Grease and flour 13×9×2-inch pan.

2. Combine dry cake mix, eggs and the amount of oil and water listed on package in large mixer bowl. Mix, bake and cool cake as directed on package. Cut cake into cubes shortly before serving.

3. For fondue, combine caramels, chocolate, milk and corn syrup in heavy saucepan. Cook over low heat, stirring constantly, until caramels and chocolate melt. Pour into fondue pot; keep warm. Add more milk if fondue becomes too thick.

4. Arrange cake cubes, marshmallows, strawberries and cherries on serving tray for dipping.

8 to 12 servings

APPLE CUSTARD DESSERT

1 package Duncan Hines
  Butter Recipe Golden
  Cake Mix
1 cup shredded or flaked
  coconut
½ cup (1 stick) butter or
  margarine

6 medium apples, pared,
  cored and cut in eighths
  (about 6 cups)
1 cup water
¼ cup lemon juice

1. Preheat oven to 350°F. Grease 13×9×2-inch baking pan.

2. Combine dry cake mix and coconut in large bowl. Cut in butter with pastry blender or two knives until crumbly.

3. Arrange apple slices in greased pan. Sprinkle crumb mixture over apples. Combine water and lemon juice; pour over all.

4. Bake at 350°F for 45 to 50 minutes or until top is lightly browned and set. Cool before serving.

12 to 16 servings

Cookies & Bars

WHEAT GERM COOKIES

1 package Duncan Hines
  Deluxe Yellow Cake Mix
1 large egg
3 tablespoons brown sugar
¼ cup Crisco Oil or Puritan
  Oil

2 tablespoons butter or
  margarine, melted
½ cup wheat germ
2 tablespoons water
½ cup chopped nuts

1. Preheat oven to 375°F.

2. Combine dry cake mix, egg, brown sugar, oil, butter, wheat germ and water in bowl. Mix with spoon. (Dough will be stiff.) Stir in nuts.

3. Drop by teaspoonfuls, 2 inches apart, on ungreased cookie sheets.

4. Bake at 375°F for 10 minutes for chewy cookies, 12 minutes for crispy cookies. Cool 1 minute on cookie sheet, then remove to rack to finish cooling.

About 3 dozen cookies

Tip: *Allow cookies to cool completely before storing. Store crisp cookies in airtight containers and chewy cookies in loosely covered containers. Never store crisp and chewy cookies in the same container.*

FROSTED COOKIES

1 package Duncan Hines
  Deluxe Fudge Marble
  Cake Mix
⅓ cup Crisco Oil or Puritan
  Oil
1 teaspoon ground ginger
2 large eggs
⅓ cup Crisco shortening

⅓ cup water
½ teaspoon salt
3 cups confectioners' sugar
1 teaspoon vanilla extract
  Milk
  Chopped nuts or coconut,
  if desired

1. Preheat oven to 350°F.

2. Combine dry cake mix, oil, ginger and eggs in bowl (do not add contents of small packet); mix well. Drop dough by teaspoonfuls onto ungreased cookie sheets.

3. Bake at 350°F for 12 to 15 minutes. Cool about 1 minute on cookie sheet, then remove to rack to finish cooling.

4. For frosting, heat shortening, water, salt and contents of small packet in saucepan until shortening melts. Remove from heat. Add confectioners' sugar and vanilla extract; beat until smooth and creamy. Add more confectioners' sugar to thicken or milk to thin as needed. Spread on cooled cookies. Sprinkle with chopped nuts or coconut. *About 4 dozen cookies*

RIBBON COOKIES

1 package Duncan Hines
  Deluxe Fudge Marble
  Cake Mix
2 large eggs

¼ teaspoon baking soda
½ cup Crisco shortening
¼ cup all-purpose flour

1. Beat eggs with baking soda in bowl. Add shortening. Blend in dry cake mix and flour; mix well (do not add contents of small packet). Divide dough in half. Blend contents of small packet into one half of dough.

2. On wax paper, shape each half of dough into a long strip ½ inch thick and ½ inches wide. Press strips together lightly. Cut to make three short strips. Wrap in wax paper and refrigerate.

3. Preheat oven to 350°F.

4. Slice dough ¼ inch thick and place on ungreased cookie sheets.

5. Bake at 350°F for 10 minutes. Cool about 1 minute on cookie sheets; remove to rack to finish cooling. *About 6 dozen cookies*

RASPBERRY OATMEAL BARS

1 package Duncan Hines
Deluxe Yellow Cake Mix
2½ cups quick-cooking oats
¾ cup (1½ sticks) butter or
margarine, melted

1 cup (12-ounce jar)
raspberry preserves or
jam*
1 tablespoon water

1. Preheat oven to 375°F. Grease 13×9×2-inch pan.

2. Combine dry cake mix and oats in large bowl; add melted butter and stir until crumbly. Measure half of crumb mixture (about 3 cups) into pan. Press firmly to cover bottom. Combine preserves and water; stir until blended. Spread over crumb mixture in pan. Sprinkle remaining crumb mixture over preserves; pat firmly to make top even.

3. Bake at 375°F for 18 to 23 minutes or until top is very light brown. Cool in pan on rack; cut into bars. Store in airtight container.

4 dozen bars

Apricot, blackberry or strawberry preserves can be substituted.

COCONUT MALLOW FUDGE SQUARES

1 package Duncan Hines
  Deluxe Devil's Food Cake
  Mix
½ cup quick-cooking oats
1 large egg, slightly beaten
½ cup Crisco Oil or Puritan
  Oil

1 package (6 ounces)
  semisweet chocolate
  pieces (1 cup)
1 package (6 ounces)
  butterscotch-flavored
  pieces (1 cup)
3 cups miniature
  marshmallows
1 cup flaked coconut

1. Preheat oven to 350°F. Grease 15½×10½×1-inch jelly roll pan.

2. Combine dry cake mix, oats, egg and oil in bowl. Mix with spoon until dry ingredients are completely moistened. Press mixture firmly and evenly into pan.

3. Bake at 350°F for 10 minutes. Remove from oven. Sprinkle chocolate pieces over crust, then butterscotch pieces, marshmallows and coconut. Bake 15 minutes more or until coconut and marshmallows just begin to brown. Cool on rack; cut into squares.

About 4 dozen squares

CARAMEL CHOCOLATE FINGERS

1 package (14 ounces)
  vanilla caramels
⅔ cup evaporated milk
1 package Duncan Hines
  Deluxe Swiss Chocolate
  Cake Mix

¾ cup (1½ sticks) butter or
  margarine, melted
1 package (6 ounces)
  semisweet chocolate
  pieces (1 cup)

1. Preheat oven to 350°F. Grease 13×9×2-inch pan.

2. Combine caramels and ⅓ cup evaporated milk in heavy saucepan. Heat and stir until blended; keep warm.

3. Combine dry cake mix, melted butter and ⅓ cup evaporated milk in bowl; mix well. Spread half of mixture in bottom of pan.

4. Bake at 350°F for 6 minutes.

5. Immediately sprinkle chocolate over hot layer; drizzle with caramel mixture. Spread remaining batter evenly over top.

6. Return to oven and bake 15 to 18 minutes more or until top looks dry. Cool on rack; cut into fingers, about 3×1 inch.

About 3 dozen bars

CREAMY CARROT CHEESE SQUARES

1 package Duncan Hines
   Deluxe Carrot Cake Mix
½ cup (1 stick) butter or
   margarine, melted
1 cup chopped pecans

2 packages (8 ounces each)
   cream cheese, softened
2 large eggs
1 teaspoon vanilla extract
20 pecan halves

1. Preheat oven to 350°F. Grease and flour 13×9×2-inch pan. Measure 1½ cups dry cake mix; set aside.

2. Combine remaining cake mix and melted butter in large mixer bowl. Mix at low speed until crumbly. Stir in chopped pecans. Press firmly into pan.

3. Bake at 350°F for 6 minutes. Cool 5 minutes, then set pan in freezer for 5 minutes or until bottom of pan is cold.

4. Beat cream cheese in large mixer bowl until smooth. Beat in reserved 1½ cups cake mix, eggs and vanilla extract. Spread over cooled crust. Arrange pecan halves on top.

5. Bake at 350°F for 23 to 28 minutes or until toothpick inserted in center comes out clean. Cool on rack. Cut into bars. Store in refrigerator.

About 20 squares

CANDY BAR COOKIES

1 package Duncan Hines
  Deluxe Yellow Cake Mix
½ cup Crisco Oil or Puritan
  Oil
1 large egg
1 package (14 ounces)
  vanilla caramels

⅓ cup evaporated milk
⅓ cup butter or margarine
1⅔ cups confectioners' sugar
1 cup chopped pecans
1 package (6 ounces)
  semisweet chocolate
  pieces (1 cup)

1. Preheat oven to 350°F.

2. For crust, combine dry cake mix, oil and egg in bowl with pastry blender. Spread evenly over bottom of ungreased 13×9×2-inch pan.

3. Bake at 350°F for 15 to 20 minutes or until light golden brown. Prepare filling while crust is baking.

4. Combine caramels and evaporated milk in top of double boiler; heat until caramels melt, stirring occasionally. Add butter; stir until melted. Remove from heat. Stir in confectioners' sugar and pecans. Spread hot caramel mixture over warm, baked crust.

5. Melt semisweet chocolate pieces over hot water in top of double boiler. Spread in very thin layer over caramel filling. Refrigerate; cut into bars when cool.   *About 4 dozen small bars*

GLAZED NUT BARS

1 package Duncan Hines
  Deluxe White Cake Mix
½ cup water
2 large eggs
¼ cup (½ stick) butter or
  margarine, softened

¼ cup packed brown sugar
1 package (6 ounces)
  semisweet chocolate
  pieces (1 cup)
½ cup chopped nuts

1. Preheat oven to 375°F. Grease and flour 13×9×2-inch pan.

2. Place dry cake mix, ¼ cup water, eggs, butter and brown sugar in large bowl. Mix thoroughly (batter will be thick). Stir in ¾ cup chocolate pieces and nuts. Turn batter into pan and spread evenly.

3. Bake at 375°F for 25 to 30 minutes or until toothpick inserted in center comes out clean. Set pan on rack.

4. Melt remaining ¼ cup chocolate pieces and remaining ¼ cup water in small saucepan. Simmer 3 minutes. Spread over warm, baked layer. Cool on rack. Cut into bars. Store in airtight container.

About 4 dozen bars

LEMON BARS

1 **package Duncan Hines**
   Deluxe Lemon Cake Mix
3 **large eggs**
⅓ **cup Crisco shortening**
½ **cup sugar**
½ **teaspoon baking powder**

¼ **teaspoon salt**
2 **teaspoons grated lemon**
   peel
¼ **cup lemon juice**
   Confectioners' sugar

1. Preheat oven to 350°F.

2. Combine dry cake mix, 1 egg and shortening in bowl; mix until crumbly. Measure 1 cup and set aside. Pat remaining mixture lightly in ungreased 13×9×2-inch pan.

3. Bake at 350°F for 15 minutes or until light brown.

4. Beat remaining two eggs, sugar, baking powder, salt, lemon peel and lemon juice until light and foamy. Pour over hot crust; sprinkle with reserved 1 cup crumb mixture.

5. Bake at 350°F for 15 minutes or until light brown. Sprinkle with confectioners' sugar. Cool on rack; cut into bars.

About 32 bars

Muffins, Loaves & Coffee Cakes

GOLDEN OATMEAL MUFFINS

1 package Duncan Hines
  Butter Recipe Golden
  Cake Mix
1 cup quick-cooking oats
¼ teaspoon salt

¾ cup milk
2 large eggs, slightly beaten
2 tablespoons butter or
  margarine, melted
  Honey or jam

1. Preheat oven to 400°F. Grease 24 muffin cups.

2. Combine dry cake mix, oats and salt in bowl. Beat together milk, eggs and butter. Add to dry ingredients, stirring just until moistened. Spoon into muffin cups, filling two-thirds full.

3. Bake at 400°F for 13 minutes or until golden brown. Serve with honey or your favorite jam.

24 muffins

Tip: *Follow the beating time indicated in the recipe or on the cake mix package, making sure you do not underbeat or overbeat. Set your kitchen timer for perfect accuracy.*

APPLE BRUNCH CAKE

1 package Duncan Hines
Butter Recipe Golden
Cake Mix
3 large eggs
½ cup (1 stick) butter or
margarine, softened
⅔ cup water

4 apples, pared, cored and
sliced (about 4 cups)
3 tablespoons sugar
4 teaspoons ground
cinnamon
Confectioners' sugar

1. Preheat oven to 375°F. Grease and flour 10-inch tube pan.

2. Combine dry cake mix, eggs, butter and water in large mixer bowl. Mix cake as directed on package. Turn two-thirds batter into pan. Toss apples with sugar and cinnamon. Spoon over batter in pan. Spread remaining batter over apples.

3. Bake at 375°F for 45 to 50 minutes or until toothpick inserted in center comes out clean. Cool in pan on rack 25 minutes. Remove from pan; cool completely on rack. Sprinkle cooled cake with confectioners' sugar.

12 to 16 servings

BLUEBERRY MUFFINS

1 package Duncan Hines
Deluxe White Cake Mix
2 tablespoons all-purpose
flour
1 teaspoon baking powder
⅔ cup milk

3 large eggs
⅓ cup Crisco Oil or Puritan
Oil
1 cup rinsed fresh or
well-drained, thawed,
frozen blueberries

1. Preheat oven to 375°F. Line 24 muffin cups with paper liners.

2. Combine dry cake mix, flour and baking powder in large bowl. Beat milk, eggs and oil together with fork; add to mixture in bowl and stir just until dry ingredients are moistened. Fold in blueberries.

3. Spoon batter into muffin cups, filling one-third full.

4. Bake at 375°F for 15 to 20 minutes or until golden brown.

24 muffins

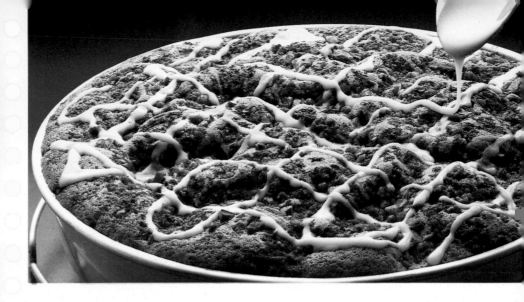

ORANGE WAKE-UP CAKE

1 package Duncan Hines
Butter Recipe Golden
Cake Mix
⅔ cup water
3 large eggs
½ cup (1 stick) butter or
margarine, softened
2 tablespoons grated orange
peel
½ cup chopped pecans

⅓ cup packed brown sugar
¼ cup fine graham cracker
crumbs
2 tablespoons butter or
margarine, melted
1½ teaspoons ground
cinnamon
1 cup confectioners' sugar
2 tablespoons hot water
¼ teaspoon vanilla extract

1. Preheat oven to 375°F. Grease and flour two 9×1½-inch round layer pans.

2. Combine dry cake mix, water, eggs and ½ cup butter in large mixer bowl. Mix cake as directed on package. Fold in 1 tablespoon of the orange peel. Divide batter evenly in pans.

3. For topping, combine pecans, brown sugar, graham cracker crumbs, 2 tablespoons butter, remaining orange peel and cinnamon; mix well. Sprinkle evenly over batter in pans.

4. Bake at 375°F for 25 to 30 minutes or until toothpick inserted in center comes out clean.

5. For glaze*, mix confectioners' sugar, hot water and vanilla until smooth. Drizzle over warm cakes. Serve warm or cool in pans.

12 to 16 servings

Or heat ⅔ cup Duncan Hines Vanilla Frosting in a small saucepan over medium heat, stirring constantly, until thin.

GOLDEN FRUIT LOAVES

1 package Duncan Hines
  Butter Recipe Golden
  Cake Mix
1½ cups chopped candied
  mixed fruit (6 ounces)
½ cup all-purpose flour

½ teaspoon baking powder
½ teaspoon baking soda
1 cup milk
2 large eggs
2 tablespoons butter or
  margarine, softened

1. Preheat oven to 350°F. Grease and flour two 8½×4½×2½-inch loaf pans.

2. Sprinkle 2 tablespoons dry cake mix over dried fruit; stir to coat.

3. Combine remaining cake mix, flour, baking powder and baking soda in large mixer bowl. Add milk, eggs and butter. Blend at low speed, then beat 2 minutes at medium speed. Fold in fruit. Divide batter evenly in pans.

4. Bake at 350°F for 45 to 50 minutes or until toothpick inserted in center comes out clean. Cool in pans on racks 20 minutes. Remove from pans; cool completely on racks.   *2 medium loaves*

CARROT MUFFINS

1 package Duncan Hines
  Deluxe Carrot Cake Mix
2 tablespoons all-purpose
  flour
1 teaspoon baking powder
¼ cup chopped nuts
⅔ cup milk
3 large eggs

⅓ cup Crisco Oil or Puritan
  Oil
6 tablespoons sugar
1 teaspoon ground
  cinnamon
¼ cup (½ stick) butter or
  margarine, melted

1. Preheat oven to 375°F. Grease 24 muffin cups or line with paper baking cups.

2. Combine dry cake mix, flour, baking powder and nuts in large bowl. Beat milk, eggs and oil together with fork in another bowl; add to dry mixture, stirring just until dry ingredients are moistened. Spoon batter into muffin cups, filling about one-third full.

3. Bake at 375°F for 15 to 20 minutes or until golden brown. Cool 5 minutes; remove from pans.

4. For topping, combine sugar and cinnamon. Dip muffin tops in melted butter and then in cinnamon-sugar.   *24 muffins*

Golden Fruit Loaves (top), Carrot Muffins (bottom)

EASY APPLE KUCHEN

2 envelopes active dry yeast	1½ cups sugar
¼ cup warm water (about 110°F)	1 tablespoon ground cinnamon
2 large eggs	⅓ cup butter or margarine
1 package Duncan Hines Deluxe Yellow Cake Mix	6 medium apples or 2 cans (20 ounces each)
1¼ cups all-purpose flour	pie-sliced apples, drained

1. Dissolve yeast in warm water in large mixer bowl. Blend in eggs and half of dry cake mix. Beat for 1 minute at medium speed. Add remaining cake mix and beat for 3 minutes at medium speed. (Batter should be quite stiff but not doughlike.) Let rest 5 minutes.

2. Sprinkle flour on board. Scrape batter out onto prepared board. Knead batter until flour is worked in, about 100 strokes. Place in greased bowl, cover, and let rise in warm, draft-free place for 30 minutes.

3. For topping, mix sugar and cinnamon in bowl; cut in butter with pastry blender or 2 knives.

4. Preheat oven to 350°F. Grease 13×9×2-inch pan and 8×8×2-inch pan. Pare, core and slice apples.

5. Punch down dough with greased fingertips. Spread dough to ¼- to ⅓-inch thickness on bottom of pans. Arrange apple slices in rows on top. Sprinkle with topping. Let rise in warm place for 30 minutes.

6. Bake at 350°F for 25 to 30 minutes or until toothpick inserted in center comes out clean. Serve warm.   *24 servings*

BANANA NUT BREAD

4 ounces cream cheese,
  softened
2 large eggs
3 medium bananas, peeled
  and mashed

1 package Duncan Hines
  Deluxe Yellow Cake Mix
¾ cup chopped nuts

1. Preheat oven to 350°F. Grease two 8½×4½×2½-inch loaf pans.

2. Put cream cheese and eggs in small mixer bowl; blend at low speed until smooth. Add mashed bananas; mix well. Place half of dry cake mix in large bowl. Add banana mixture and beat until blended. Add remaining cake mix and nuts; stir just until blended. Divide batter evenly in pans.

3. Bake at 350°F for 35 to 45 minutes or until toothpick inserted in center comes out clean. Cool in pans on racks 20 minutes. Remove from pans; cool completely on racks.

2 medium loaves

APPLE RAISIN MUFFINS

1 package Duncan Hines
  Deluxe Apple Cake Mix
2 tablespoons all-purpose
  flour
1 teaspoon baking powder
⅔ cup milk

3 large eggs
⅓ cup Crisco Oil or Puritan
  Oil
½ cup chopped apple
½ cup chopped raisins

1. Preheat oven to 375°F. Line 24 muffin cups with paper baking cups.

2. Combine dry cake mix, flour and baking powder in large bowl. Beat milk, eggs and oil together with fork; add to mixture in bowl and stir until dry ingredients are moistened. Fold in chopped apple and raisins. Spoon batter into muffin cups, filling about two-thirds full.

3. Bake at 375°F for 15 to 20 minutes or until golden brown.

24 muffins

APPLE OATMEAL LOAF

1 package Duncan Hines
   Deluxe Apple Cake Mix
½ cup plus 2 tablespoons
   quick-cooking oats

3 large eggs
⅓ cup Crisco Oil or Puritan
   Oil
1¼ cups water

1. Preheat oven to 350°F. Grease and flour 9×5×3-inch loaf pan.

2. Combine dry cake mix, ½ cup oats, eggs, oil and water in large mixer bowl. Mix cake as directed on package. Turn batter into pan. Sprinkle with remaining 2 tablespoons oats.

3. Bake at 350°F for 55 to 65 minutes or until toothpick inserted in center comes out clean. Cool in pan on rack 15 to 20 minutes. Remove from pan; cool completely on rack.

1 large loaf

APRICOT STREUSEL COFFEE CAKE

1 package Duncan Hines
   Deluxe Yellow Cake Mix
3 large eggs
⅓ cup Crisco Oil or Puritan
   Oil
1 cup water

2 cans (16 ounces each)
   apricot halves, drained
2 teaspoons ground
   cinnamon
1 teaspoon ground nutmeg
3 tablespoons brown sugar

1. Preheat oven to 350°F. Grease and flour 13×9×2-inch pan. Measure 2 tablespoons dry cake mix and set aside.

2. Combine remaining dry cake mix, eggs, oil and water in large mixer bowl. Mix cake as directed on package. Turn batter into pan and spread evenly.

3. Arrange drained apricot halves in rows on top of batter. Combine 2 tablespoons reserved cake mix, cinnamon, nutmeg and brown sugar. Sprinkle mixture over apricots.

4. Bake at 350°F for 40 to 45 minutes or until toothpick inserted in center comes out clean. Allow cake to cool 1 hour on rack before serving.

16 servings

Apple Oatmeal Loaf

BANANA MUFFINS

1 package Duncan Hines
  Deluxe Banana Cake Mix
2 tablespoons all-purpose
  flour
1 teaspoon baking powder

¼ cup chopped nuts
¾ cup plus 2 tablespoons
  milk
2 large eggs

1. Preheat oven to 375°F. Grease 24 muffin cups or line with paper baking cups.

2. Combine dry cake mix, flour, baking powder and nuts in large bowl. Beat milk and eggs together with fork; add to mixture in bowl and stir just until dry ingredients are moistened.

3. Spoon batter into muffin cups, filling one-third full.

4. Bake at 375°F for 15 to 20 minutes or until golden brown.

24 muffins

SOUR CREAM BRUNCH CAKE

1 package Duncan Hines
  Deluxe Yellow Cake Mix
1 cup dairy sour cream
4 large eggs
½ cup Crisco Oil or Puritan
  Oil
1 package (4-serving-
  size) vanilla instant
  pudding and pie filling mix

2 teaspoons vanilla extract
⅓ cup sugar
1 teaspoon unsweetened
  cocoa
1 teaspoon ground
  cinnamon
½ cup chopped nuts

1. Preheat oven to 350°F. Grease and flour 10-inch tube pan.

2. Combine dry cake mix, sour cream, eggs, oil, pudding mix and vanilla extract in large mixer bowl. Beat 4 minutes at medium speed. Turn half of batter into pan.

3. Combine sugar, cocoa, cinnamon and nuts. Sprinkle half of cocoa mixture over batter in pan. Add remaining batter and sprinkle with remaining topping.

4. Bake at 350°F for 50 to 55 minutes or until toothpick inserted in center comes out clean. Cool cake completely on rack before removing from pan.

12 to 16 servings

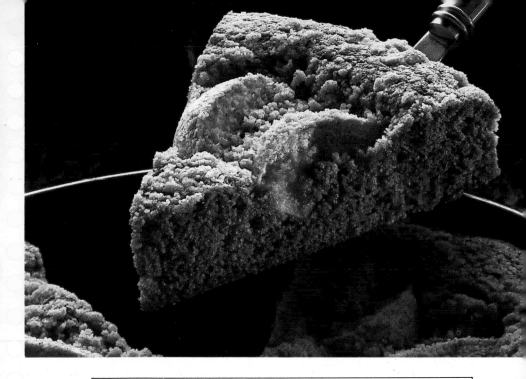

CARROT APPLE STREUSEL CAKE

1 package Duncan Hines
  Deluxe Carrot Cake Mix
1¾ teaspoons ground
  cinnamon
3 large eggs, slightly beaten
½ cup applesauce
⅓ cup Crisco Oil or Puritan
  Oil

3 baking apples, pared,
  cored, and cut into eighths
½ cup all-purpose flour
2 tablespoons sugar
¼ cup (½ stick) butter or
  margarine

1. Preheat oven to 350°F. Grease and flour two 9×1½-inch round layer pans.

2. Combine dry cake mix and ½ teaspoon cinnamon in large bowl. Combine eggs, applesauce and oil; add to dry ingredients and mix thoroughly with wooden spoon. Divide batter evenly in pans. Arrange sliced apples on top.

3. For streusel, combine flour, sugar and 1¼ teaspoons cinnamon in small bowl. Cut in butter with pastry blender or 2 knives until crumbly. Sprinkle evenly over apples.

4. Bake at 350°F for 28 to 33 minutes or until toothpick inserted in center comes out clean. Cool in pan 10 minutes. Serve warm.

12 to 16 servings

Index

A

Angel Food Cake Mix
Cinnamon Ripple Cake, 29
Coffee Cream Angel Cake, 18
Elegant Angel Torte, 16
Peanut Butter Angel Roll, 34
Strawberries Romanoff on Angel
Slices, 12
Angel Food Cake Tips, 7
Apple(s)
Brunch Cake, 84
Cake, French, 37
Cake, Swedish, 67
Custard Dessert, 73
Kuchen, Easy, 88
Oatmeal Loaf, 90
Raisin Muffins, 89
Streusel Cake, Carrot, 93
Apple Cake Mix
Apple Oatmeal Loaf, 90
Apple Raisin Muffins, 89
Apricot(s)
Layer, Glazed, 21
Streusel Coffee Cake, 90
Supreme Cake, 19

B

Back-to-School Pencil Cake, 48
Baking Cakes, 3
Banana(s)
Cupcakes, Fudge 'N', 52
Muffins, 92
Nut Bread, 89
Split Cakes, 23
Banana Cake Mix
Banana Muffins, 92
Bars
Candy Bar Cookies, 80
Caramel Chocolate Fingers, 78
Christmas Fruit, 62
Glazed Nut, 80
Lemon, 81
Raspberry Oatmeal, 77
Birthday Cakelets, 50
Blueberry Muffins, 84
Breads (*see also* Coffee Cakes,
Muffins)
Apple Oatmeal Loaf, 90
Banana Nut, 89
Golden Fruit Loaves, 86
Butter Recipe Fudge Cake Mix
Sweet Chocolate Mousse Cake, 14
Butter Recipe Golden Cake Mix
Apple Brunch Cake, 84

continued
Apple Custard Dessert, 73
Golden Crunch Cake, 26
Golden Fruit Loaves, 86
Golden Oatmeal Muffins, 83
Holiday Coffee Cake, 58
Orange Wake-Up Cake, 85
Sock-It-To-Me Cake, 36
Viennese Cherry Cheese Torte, 15

C

Candy Bar Cookies, 80
Caramel(s)
Candy Bar Cookies, 80
Chocolate Fingers, 78
Fondue Party, 72
Carrot Apple Streusel Cake, 93
Carrot Cake Mix
Carrot Apple Streusel Cake, 93
Carrot Cake Supreme, 31
Carrot Muffins, 86
Creamy Carrot Cheese Squares, 79
Nutty Crunch Cake, 41
Peach Carrot Cheesecake, 65
Carrot Cake Supreme, 31
Carrot Muffins, 86
Cheesecake
Chocolate Swirl, 70
Peach Carrot, 65
Cherry
Cake Cobbler, 69
Cheese Torte, Viennese, 15
Dump Cake, 24
Fruit 'N' Cream Squares, 71
Nut Cake, 35
Torte, Chocolate, 20
Cherry Cake Mix
Cherry Nut Cake, 35
Chocolat au Rhum, 17
Chocolate
Birthday Cakelets, 50
Cake, Easy German, 30
Cherry Torte, 20
Chocolat au Rhum, 17
Coconut Mallow Fudge Squares, 78
Crumb Pie, 68
Cupcake Cones, 53
Fingers, Caramel, 78
Fondue Party, 72
Fruit Cake, 56
Fudge 'N' Banana Cupcakes, 52
Mocha Charmer, 25
Mousse Cake, Sweet, 14
New Orleans Crumb Cake, 33

continued
Open House Ribbon Torte, 11
Party Cake, Luscious, 9
Refrigerator Dessert, 66
Swirl Cheesecake, 70
Toasty Topped Cake Slices, 39
Zucchini Cake, 40
Chocolate Chip Cake Mix
Banana Split Cakes, 23
Chocolate Zucchini Cake, 40
Christmas Fruit Bars, 62
Cinnamon Ripple Cake, 29
Cobbler
Cherry Cake, 69
Thanksgiving Cranberry, 57
Coconut
Apple Custard Dessert, 73
Cherry Nut Cake, 35
Crisps, 60
Easy German Chocolate Cake, 30
Glazed Apricot Layer, 21
Mallow Fudge Squares, 78
Coffee Cake
Apple Brunch Cake, 84
Apricot Streusel, 90
Carrot Apple Streusel Cake, 93
Easy Apple Kuchen, 88
Holiday, 58
Orange Wake-Up Cake, 85
Sour Cream Brunch Cake, 92
Coffee Cream Angel Cake, 18
Cookies
Coconut Crisps, 60
Frosted, 76
Gingerbread People, 58
Jelly Jewels, 60
Ribbon, 76
Wheat Germ, 75
Cranberry Cobbler, Thanksgiving, 57
Creamy Carrot Cheese Squares, 79
Cupcake(s)
Cones, 53
Fudge 'N' Banana, 52
Mister Funny Face, 43

D

Decorating Cakes, 5
Deep Chocolate Cake Mix
Chocolate Zucchini Cake, 40
Devil's Food Cake Mix
Birthday Cakelets, 50
Chocolat au Rhum, 17
Chocolate Cherry Torte, 20
Chocolate Fruit Cake, 56
Chocolate Swirl Cheesecake, 70
Coconut Mallow Fudge Squares, 78
Cupcake Cones, 53
Fudge 'N' Banana Cupcakes, 52

continued
Luscious Chocolate Party Cake, 9
New Orleans Crumb Cake, 33
Dump Cake, 24

E

Easy Apple Kuchen, 88
Easy German Chocolate Cake, 30
Elegant Angel Torte, 16

F

Fondue Party, 72
Freezing & Thawing, 7
French Apple Cake, 37
Frosted Cookies, 76
Frosting Cakes, 5
Fruit Cake
Chocolate, 56
Holiday, 63
Fudge Marble Cake Mix
Chocolate Crumb Pie, 68
Frosted Cookies, 76
Open House Ribbon Torte, 11
Ribbon Cookies, 76
Fudge 'N' Banana Cupcakes, 52

G

Gingerbread People, 58
Glazed Apricot Layer, 21
Glazed Nut Bars, 80
Golden Crunch Cake, 26
Golden Fruit Loaves, 86
Golden Oatmeal Muffins, 83

H

High altitude baking, 6
Holiday Coffee Cake, 58
Holiday Fruit Cake, 63
Hopscotch Cake, 49

I

Ice Cream Cone Cakes, 46

J

Jelly Jewels, 60

L

Lemon Bars, 81
Lemon Cake Mix
Lemon Bars, 81
Lemon Pear Upside-Down Cake, 26
Swedish Apple Cake, 67
Lemon Pear Upside-Down Cake, 26
Luscious Chocolate Party Cake, 9

M

Mister Funny Face, 43
Mocha Charmer, 25

Muffins
    Apple Raisin, 89
    Banana, 92
    Blueberry, 84
    Carrot. 86
    Golden Oatmeal, 83

N

New Orleans Crumb Cake, 33
Nutty Crunch Cake, 41

O

Oatmeal
    Bars, Raspberry, 77
    Loaf, Apple, 90
    Muffins, Golden, 83
Open House Ribbon Torte, 11
Orange Cake Mix
    Orange Cinnamon Tea Cake, 38
    Raisin-Filled Orange Cake, 28
Orange Cinnamon Tea Cake, 38
Orange Wake-Up Cake, 85

P

Peach(es)
    Carrot Cheesecake, 65
    Thanksgiving Cranberry Cobbler, 57
Peanut Butter
    Angel Roll, 34
    Nutty Crunch Cake, 41
    Teddy Bear Cake, 44
Pear Upside-Down Cake, Lemon, 26
Pie, Chocolate Crumb, 68
Pineapple
    Blitz Torte, 10
    Carrot Cake Supreme, 31
    Christmas Tree Cake, 55
    Dump Cake, 24
Pineapple Cake Mix
    Pineapple Blitz Torte, 10
    Pineapple Christmas Tree Cake, 55

R

Raisin-Filled Orange Cake, 28
Raisin Muffins, Apple, 89
Raspberry Oatmeal Bars, 77
Rhubarb-Sauced Strawberry Cake, 32
Ribbon Cookies, 76

S

Sock-It-To-Me Cake, 36
Sour Cream Brunch Cake, 92
Spice Cake Mix
    Gingerbread People, 58
    Holiday Fruit Cake, 63
Storing Cakes, 6
Strawberries
    Fondue Party, 72
    Mister Funny Face, 43

continued
    Romanoff on Angel Slices, 12
Strawberry Cake Mix
    Rhubarb-Sauce Strawberry Cake, 32
Swedish Apple Cake, 67
Sweet Chocolate Mousse Cake, 14
Swiss Chocolate Cake Mix
    Caramel Chocolate Fingers, 78
    Chocolate Refrigerator Dessert, 66
    Easy German Chocolate Cake, 30
    Mocha Charmer, 25

T

Teddy Bear Cake, 44
Thanksgiving Cranberry Cobbler, 57
Tips for Angel Food Cake, 7
Toasty Topped Cake Slices, 39
Tortes
    Chocolate Cherry, 20
    Elegant Angel, 16
    Open House Ribbon, 11
    Pineapple Blitz, 10
    Viennese Cherry Cheese, 15

V

Viennese Cherry Cheese Torte, 15

W

Wheat Germ Cookies, 75
White Cake Mix
    Apricot Supreme Cake, 19
    Blueberry Muffins, 84
    Cherry Cake Cobbler, 69
    French Apple Cake, 37
    Glazed Nut Bars, 80
    Mister Funny Face, 43

Y

Yellow Cake Mix
    Apricot Streusel Coffee Cake, 90
    Banana Nut Bread, 89
    Candy Bar Cookies, 80
    Cherry Fruit 'N' Cream Squares, 71
    Christmas Fruit Bars, 62
    Coconut Crisps, 60
    Dump Cake, 24
    Easy Apple Kuchen, 88
    Glazed Apricot Layer, 21
    Hopscotch Cake, 49
    Jelly Jewels, 60
    Rapsberry Oatmeal Bars, 77
    Sour Cream Brunch Cake, 92
    Thanksgiving Cranberry Cobbler, 57
    Toasty Topped Cake Slices, 39
    Wheat Germ Cookies, 75

Z

Zucchini Cake, Chocolate, 40